Sistah's Are You Listening?

An Empowerment Guide For Black Women From A Black Male Life Coach

Coach Michael Taylor

Published by Creation Publishing Group LLC
www.creationpublishing.com
© 2024 Michael Taylor
ISBN # 978-1-7366369-5-4

Library of Congress Number # 2022902295

All rights reserved. No part of this book may be used, reproduced, stored in or introduced into a retrieval system, or transmitted in any form or by any means without the express written consent of the publisher.

Published and printed in the United States of America.

About Coach Michael Taylor

Michael Taylor is a shining example of resilience and determination, having overcome immense personal challenges to become a renowned life coach, motivational speaker, and bestselling author. His unwavering commitment to empowering others has inspired countless individuals to pursue their dreams and live extraordinary lives.

A former high school dropout, Michael faced seemingly insurmountable obstacles, including divorce, bankruptcy, foreclosure, depression, and even homelessness. Yet, through sheer grit and an unshakable belief in himself, he emerged from these trials as a beacon of hope and inspiration.

With 14 published books under his belt, Michael's words have touched the lives of readers worldwide, guiding them towards personal growth, self-discovery, and the realization of their full potential. As a certified life coach, he has dedicated his life to helping men and women break free from self-imposed limitations and embrace the extraordinary within themselves.

Michael's journey has been a testament to the power of perseverance and the indomitable human spirit. As the president and CEO of Creation Publishing Group, he continues to champion the pursuit of dreams and the creation of a life filled with purpose and fulfillment.

Happily married to his soulmate, Bedra, for over two decades, Michael finds solace and joy in the simple pleasures of life. When he's not empowering others through his writing and coaching, you'll find him indulging in the soulful melodies of 70s and 80s music or immersing himself in the latest cinematic masterpieces.

With an infectious optimism and an unwavering passion for the impossible, Michael Taylor stands as a testament to the boundless potential that lies within each of us. He firmly believes that there has never been a better time to be alive on this planet, and his mission is to inspire others to embrace this belief and live their lives to the fullest.

Table of contents

About Coach Michael Taylor iii

Acknowledgements vii

Introduction 1

Chapter 1: Cultural Conditioning 5
Chapter 2: Shattering Black Women Stereotypes 25
Chapter 3: Healing 45
Chapter 4: There Are Lots Of Good Men 65
Chapter 5: Relationships 79
Chapter 6: Healthy Sexuality 99
Chapter 7: Creating Dynamic Health 117
Chapter 8: Spirituality 135
Chapter 9: Get Your Mind Right To Get Your Money Right ... 155
Chapter 10: Be Willing To Serve 175
Bio 193

Acknowledgements

First, foremost, and always, I must acknowledge the Source of my inspiration for writing this book. It is my belief there is a divine intelligence that created and is still creating this amazing Universe we live in. Some people use the word God to describe and define it but I do not believe the word you use really matters. Some people use the word Yahweh, others say Great Spirit, some use the term Creator, while others may say The Universe, but ultimately, the word isn't important. What's important is to develop an intimacy and connection to this power which is greater than yourself and to recognize it as the "Source" of all things. I know with absolute certainty that this "Source" is where my inspiration for writing this book comes from and therefore, I am acknowledging my Source for giving me the inspiration and the wisdom to share the insights contained within this book.

So, thank you God, for using me as a conduit to share your wisdom with the women (and men) who will be reading this book.

~~~~~~~~~~~~

I would be remiss to write a book for black women if I didn't begin by acknowledging the most amazing black woman I know, my mom Geneva. My mom is the epitome of an intelligent, loving, caring, and strong black woman. At one point in her life she would have been considered the poster child for poverty. She was a single mother raising six children back in the sixties living in government housing on government assistance. Despite seemingly insurmountable odds, she was able to overcome a multitude of adversities to pull herself out of poverty and raise her children to become productive members of society.

As I reflect over my own life, I realize that everything I am I owe to her. Through her actions she taught me resilience, persistence, commitment, patience, and faith. I would not be who I am, and where I am, without her love, guidance and support. Of all the lessons she taught me, the one that stands out the most is this; "if you want something badly enough, there is no one or no thing that can keep you from attaining it except yourself"

Thank you mom for being such an inspiration and role model of positivity for me. Your love and guidance has inspired me to dream big and not let anything or anyone keep me from fulfilling my divine purpose.

I love you!

~~~~~~~~~~~~

I must give a shoutout to my baby girl Katrina. Words cannot express just how proud I am of the incredible woman you grew into. I am inspired as I see you traveling the world living your best life while also being a big sister and mentor for young black women. You are definitely a role model for black women and I am extremely grateful that I get to call you my baby girl no matter how old you get.

I love you to the moon and back and am so very proud of you!

~~~~~~~~~~~~~~

As I put together the content for this book I must admit that my wife is one of the reasons I decided to write it. First of all, she insisted that I write a book for black women since the majority of my books are targeted to black men, and secondly, she is definitely the type of woman who exudes the content of this book as an amazing black woman. We have been happily married for 22 years now and I can honestly say they have been the happiest years of my life. From our very first date I knew she had the potential to become the perfect life partner for me. Within 6 months I knew I wanted to spend the rest of my life with her because we shared the same qualities and values in the most important areas of life. She is without question my ride or die mate and I count my blessings to have her in my life.

So here's to you Mrs. B! Thank you for being the amazing woman that you are and for being my life partner who I get to share life with.

I'm looking forward to the next 40-50 years with you!

Introduction

Contrary to mainstream media, it is my belief there has never been a better time to be alive on the planet than right now. I realize I may be in the minority with that statement because of all of the negativity and pessimism of our media, but, I firmly believe our best days are ahead of us not behind us as a human species and I am committed to doing my part in ensuring this is true.

As our country continues to grapple with racial conflict and division, I still remain optimistic that the future is bright when it comes to the future of race relations. However, what I have noticed is a lack of resources specifically for black men and women who are committed to their personal growth and development and so I have made it my life's work to provide those resources for the men and women who are seeking them.

As a man who happens to be black, I've made it my life's work to empower black men to build extraordinary lives, and as a certified life coach, I provide them with some tools to do this. Over the past 25-30 years I've written several books dealing with black male empowerment and the changing roles of manhood and masculinity and I've inspired men around the globe with my books, lectures, workshops, and podcasts. My intention is to create a new paradigm of masculinity in which men embrace new ways of being and relating as men. In doing so, I believe I can help eradicate a large percentage of social ills that currently plague our world.

So why write a book for black women?

Great question, so let me jump right in.

As a life coach, I have come to know that men and women really want the same things. We both want to have inner peace, dynamic health, great relationships, financial abundance and a sense of fulfillment and purpose. I have helped countless men experience these things and I'm certain the wisdom I share in this book will help women accomplish those things also. I also believe that the key to resolving a lot of the challenges facing the black community is to strengthen family units, and one way to do this is to make sure the men and women have invested in their emotional, psychological, intellectual, and spiritual development. Put another way, we must each begin our own individual journey of transformatioen that challenges us to heal our hearts, make peace with our pasts, and find our divine purpose, in doing so, we lay the foundation for the transformation of our communities and our world.

This is what I'm committed to. Sharing the knowledge and wisdom I've gained through my own personal journey with others in an effort to help make the world a better place.

I believe this empowerment guide for black women can do just that. Empower them to reach their full potential and build the life of their dreams, while making the world a better place, because ultimately, isn't that what we all want?

Sistah's are you listening?

The time is now to build the life of your dreams, and this empowerment guide can help you do that.

Good luck!

Michael

"*We have to talk about liberating minds as well as liberating society.*"
— Angela Davis

CHAPTER 1

Cultural Conditioning

Embracing Your Identity

As a Black woman, navigating the intricacies of identity is an ongoing and multifaceted journey that requires a deep introspection into the intersections of race, gender, and class. Embracing your identity means embracing the complexities of being part of a community that is both resilient and diverse, yet often marginalized and oppressed by systemic injustices. It entails an unwavering commitment to challenging societal norms and stereotypes while celebrating the richness and vibrancy of Black cultures.

Being a Black woman means recognizing the historical legacy of strength and resistance that has been handed down through generations, from the fierce activism of Harriet Tubman and Sojourner Truth to the groundbreaking achievements of figures like Audre Lorde and Maya Angelou. It means acknowledging the impact of colonization, slavery, and racism on the construction of Black female identity and reclaiming space for your voice to be heard and your experiences to be validated.

Embracing your identity as a Black woman involves a deep sense of connection to your roots, your ancestors, and the stories that have shaped your existence. It means grappling with the stereotypes and biases that society imposes on you, from the hypersexualization of Black women to the erasure of their intellectual contributions. It requires an active dismantling of these harmful narratives and a refusal to be defined by anyone else's limited perceptions of who you are.

In embracing your identity, you are not only asserting your right to exist authentically but also demanding recognition for the fullness of your humanity. It is a radical act of self-love and defiance, a refusal to conform to society's expectations and a commitment to carving out a space where your voice, your experiences, and your worth are seen and valued.

Embracing your identity as a Black woman is a revolutionary act, a testament to the resilience, creativity, and beauty that have flourished in the face of centuries of oppression. It is a call to action to dismantle the systems of power that seek to silence you and a testament to the power of community, solidarity, and collective resistance. Embrace your identity with strength, with pride, and with the knowledge that you are a force to be reckoned with in a world that often seeks to diminish your light.

Finding Your Voice

In a world that often tries to silence marginalized voices, finding your voice as a Black woman is a profound and transformative journey that goes beyond mere self-expression. It is an act of defiance against a society that seeks to diminish and erase your identity, a reclaiming of your power and agency in a world that seeks to silence you.

Finding your voice as a Black woman means acknowledging the intersectionality of your identity – the unique combination of race, gender, and other facets that shape your experiences and perspectives. It is recognizing that your voice carries the weight of centuries of oppression and resilience, of struggle and triumph, of sorrow and joy.

To find your voice, you must navigate a complex landscape of expectations, stereotypes, and biases that seek to confine and limit you. It is a process of breaking free from the chains of Eurocentric standards of beauty, behavior, and success, and embracing your own truth, your own story, your own worth.

To speak as a Black woman is to speak from a place of deep-rooted strength and resilience, forged through generations of struggle and resistance. It is to honor the legacy of those who came before you, who fought for justice and equality, and to carry their spirit and determination in your words and actions.

In finding your voice, you embrace the fullness of your identity, celebrating the richness of your culture, heritage, and experiences. You refuse to be silenced or sidelined, demanding to be seen, heard, and valued for who you truly are.

Finding your voice as a Black woman is not just about speaking up – it is about creating space for your voice to be heard, respected, and uplifted. It is about challenging systems of oppression and advocating for change, not just for yourself, but for all those who are marginalized and silenced.

In the journey to find your voice, you discover the power and beauty of your own truth, and you stand boldly and unapologetically in your authenticity. Your voice becomes a beacon of hope, a call to action, a force for transformation in a world that desperately needs to hear and heed your message.

Finding your voice is a journey that requires courage, resilience, and a deep sense of self-awareness. It is a process of unearthing layers of conditioning and societal expectations to reveal the core of your authentic self. As a Black woman, this journey is often fraught with unique challenges and complexities stemming from the intersections of race, gender, and other aspects of identity.

To find your voice is to confront the legacy of historical trauma and systemic injustices that continue to shape your experiences and shape societal perceptions of who you are. It is an act of reclaiming your narrative, rewriting the script that has been imposed upon you, and asserting your right to define yourself on your own terms.

In the process of finding your voice, you may encounter resistance, both internal and external. You may grapple with self-doubt, societal pressures, and the fear of speaking out against systems of power that seek to silence you. But through this struggle, you cultivate a sense of inner strength and resilience that allows you to push past these barriers and stand firmly in your truth.

Your voice as a Black woman holds immense power – the power to challenge ingrained biases, dismantle stereotypes, and inspire others to embrace their own authenticity. It is a force of empowerment, a catalyst for change, and a testament to the beauty and strength of Black womanhood.

In finding your voice, you not only empower yourself but also contribute to the collective empowerment of all Black women. Your voice becomes a part of a rich tapestry of stories, experiences, and perspectives that collectively challenge the status quo and pave the way for a more inclusive and just society.

As you continue on your journey of finding your voice, remember that your words have the potential to spark revolutions, ignite change, and build bridges between communities. Embrace the power of your voice, speak your truth boldly and unapologetically, and know that your voice matters – now and always.

Breaking Through Barriers

In a world where barriers seem to perpetually inhibit progress and success, the journey for Black women to break through these obstacles is one filled with resilience, determination, and unwavering strength.

As Black women navigate their paths, they often encounter systemic racism, gender discrimination, and societal biases that seek to limit their opportunities and stunt their growth. These barriers can manifest in various ways, from unequal pay in the workplace to limited access to resources and opportunities for advancement. The intersectionality of being both Black and female creates a unique set of challenges that amplify the obstacles they face, requiring them to navigate a complex web of discrimination and marginalization.

Despite these challenges, Black women have continued to rise above adversity, carving out their own paths to success and shattering glass ceilings along the way. By leveraging their unique perspectives, talents, and experiences, they challenge the status quo and redefine what is possible for themselves and future generations. Through their perseverance, Black women not only defy stereotypes and expectations but also inspire others to push boundaries and strive for excellence in the face of adversity.

Breaking through barriers is not merely about overcoming external challenges; it is also a journey of self-discovery and empowerment. Black women learn to embrace their identities, cultivate their strengths, and stand firm in their convictions, refusing to be defined by society's limitations. They draw strength from their heritage, ancestors, and communities, recognizing the legacy of resilience and resistance that has been passed down through generations.

Through resilience, perseverance, and a steadfast belief in their own worth, Black women forge their own destinies and pave the way for a future where barriers are dismantled, and equality reigns supreme. They inspire others to follow in their footsteps, showing that with determination and courage, any obstacle can be overcome. In pushing against the constraints that seek to hold them back, Black women embody the spirit of perseverance and resilience that serves as a beacon of hope and inspiration for all who seek to defy the odds and make their mark on the world.

In breaking through barriers, Black women demonstrate the power of resilience, the beauty of diversity, and the limitless potential that lies within each of them. Their stories are a testament to the strength of the human spirit and a reminder that no obstacle is insurmountable when faced with unwavering determination and a fierce sense of purpose.

When Black women face challenges in their personal and professional lives, they often draw from a wellspring of inner strength that has been cultivated through generations of resilience and determination. This reservoir of strength allows them to navigate the complexities of racism, sexism, and other forms of discrimination with grace and fortitude, never backing down in the face of adversity. Their ability to persevere in the face of hardship is a testament to their unwavering spirit and the legacy of survival that has been passed down through the ages.

Moreover, Black women's journeys to success are often not solitary endeavors but are deeply intertwined with their communities and support networks. They understand the importance of lifting as they climb, extending a helping hand to others who may be facing similar challenges and obstacles. By sharing their stories, offering mentorship, and advocating for change, Black women create a ripple effect that empowers not only themselves but also those around them. This sense of community and solidarity propels them forward, amplifying their voices and impact in a world that often seeks to silence them.

In breaking through barriers, Black women not only defy the odds but also pave the way for a more equitable and just society for all. Their resilience, perseverance, and unwavering commitment to creating change serve as a beacon of hope and inspiration for all who dare to dream beyond the confines of limitations. Through their courage and determination, Black women rewrite the narrative of what is possible, challenging preconceived notions and setting a new standard for excellence and empowerment.

Navigating Racism and Discrimination

Navigating Racism and Discrimination:

As a Black woman, navigating racism and discrimination is a complex and multifaceted experience deeply embedded in the fabric of society. The layers of oppression that they face extend beyond individual interactions to encompass systemic inequalities that permeate every aspect of their lives. From the criminal justice system to education, employment, housing, healthcare, and beyond, the impact of racism and discrimination is wide-reaching and pervasive.

Microaggressions, subtle slights, and overt acts of racism are daily occurrences that chip away at their sense of self-worth and belonging. These acts serve to reinforce harmful stereotypes and perpetuate the dehumanization of Black women. It is crucial to recognize the insidious nature of these microaggressions and to challenge them whenever possible, both for themselves and for future generations who deserve to live in a world free from prejudice and discrimination.

At the intersection of race and gender, Black women face unique challenges that often go unrecognized or unaddressed. The stereotypes of the "angry Black woman" or the hypersexualized "Jezebel" serve to further marginalize and limit their opportunities for advancement and success. It is essential to confront and dismantle these harmful narratives, both within themselves and in the broader society, in order to create a more equitable and inclusive world for all.

Finding a support system of like-minded individuals who understand and validate their experiences is a critical component of navigating racism and discrimination. Building a community of solidarity and mutual respect can provide a sense of belonging and empowerment that helps counteract the feelings of isolation and invisibility that often accompany experiences of prejudice and bias.

Self-care practices take on added importance in the face of racism and discrimination. Engaging in activities that nourish the soul, seeking therapy or counseling to process trauma and build resilience, and cultivating a sense of inner peace and strength through mindfulness and meditation are vital tools for maintaining emotional and mental well-being in the midst of adversity.

Advocacy is a powerful tool for effecting change and challenging systemic injustices. By using their voices to speak out against racism and discrimination, sharing their stories, and amplifying the voices of others, they can contribute to a more just and inclusive society for all. It is through their collective efforts that they can begin to dismantle the oppressive structures that perpetuate inequality and create a world where Black women are truly seen, heard, and valued for who they are.

In the face of racism and discrimination, remember that you are not alone. You are part of a resilient and vibrant community of Black women who have been navigating these challenges for generations. Lean on your support system, prioritize self-care, and advocate for change. You have the strength and courage to navigate these obstacles and emerge stronger on the other side.

Expanding on this topic further, it is important to acknowledge the intergenerational trauma that can impact Black women's experiences of racism and discrimination. Historical injustices, such as slavery, segregation, and systemic racism, have left a legacy of pain and suffering that continues to reverberate through our communities today. This inherited trauma can manifest in various ways, from feelings of powerlessness and anger to struggles with mental health and emotional well-being.

Additionally, the intersectionality of identities must be considered when discussing the experiences of Black women in navigating racism and discrimination. Black women who also identify as LGBTQ+, disabled, immigrant, or belonging to other marginalized groups may face compounded forms of oppression that further complicate their experiences. Intersectional approaches to advocacy and activism are crucial in addressing the diverse needs and challenges faced by individuals with multiple marginalized identities.

Education and awareness are key components in combating racism and discrimination. By learning about the history of racial oppression, examining their own biases and privileges, and actively seeking out diverse perspectives, they can work towards creating a more equitable and inclusive society. It is important to engage in uncomfortable conversations, challenge racist attitudes and behaviors, and support initiatives that promote diversity, equity, and inclusion in all spheres of society.

In the realm of mental health, the impacts of racism and discrimination cannot be understated. The chronic stress, trauma, and societal marginalization experienced by Black women can take a significant toll on mental well-being. Seeking out culturally competent mental health professionals, engaging in healing practices rooted in their cultural traditions, and advocating for mental health resources tailored to the specific needs of Black women are crucial steps in promoting holistic health and wellness.

Ultimately, the journey of navigating racism and discrimination as a Black woman is one that requires resilience, strength, and a deep commitment to social justice. By amplifying their voices, sharing their stories, and standing in solidarity with one another, they can continue to push back against systems of oppression and work towards a more just and equitable world for all. Their experiences are valid, their voices are powerful, and their collective movement towards equality and liberation is unstoppable.

Cultivating Resilience and Strength

In a world that often seeks to diminish their worth and undermine their achievements, Black women must cultivate resilience and strength to navigate the challenges they face. Their journey towards self-empowerment is not always easy, but it is essential in overcoming adversity and standing tall in the face of injustice.

Resilience is a quality deeply ingrained in the fabric of Black womanhood, rooted in the history of their ancestors who endured unimaginable hardships with unwavering courage and determination. From the days of slavery to the civil rights movement and beyond, Black women have been at the forefront of the fight for equality, facing systemic oppression and discrimination with a resilience that transcends generations.

This resilience is not just a passive acceptance of adversity but a powerful force that enables Black women to transform their pain into purpose, their struggles into strength. It is the ability to adapt, to bounce back from setbacks, and to find creative solutions to the challenges they face. Resilience is a testament to the indomitable spirit of Black women, a testament to their ability to rise above circumstances and create change in the face of adversity.

Strength, on the other hand, is a multifaceted quality that encompasses physical, mental, and emotional fortitude. It is the inner power that allows Black women to stand firm in their convictions, to speak truth to power, and to resist the forces that seek to diminish their worth. Strength is not just about physical prowess but about the courage to confront their fears, the resilience to weather storms, and the wisdom to know when to stand up and when to stand down.

In cultivating resilience and strength, Black women must also prioritize self-care and self-love. In a society that often devalues and marginalizes their voices, it is essential to nurture their own well-being in order to continue advocating for justice and equality. This means setting boundaries, practicing self-care rituals, and surrounding themselves with a community that uplifts and supports them in their journey towards empowerment.

As Black women continue to navigate the complexities of a world that seeks to silence them, it is their resilience and strength that sustain them and propel them forward. By embracing these qualities, they honor the legacy of those who came before them and pave the way for future generations of Black women to follow in their footsteps, standing tall in the face of adversity and forging a path towards a more just and equitable world for all.

Black women carry within them a resilience that is as ancient as the roots of the baobab tree, stretching down deep into the soil of our collective history. Ancestors who bore the weight of chains and lashes, who stood strong in the face of unimaginable horrors, their spirits still echoing in the chambers of their hearts. It is their resilience that courses through their veins, empowering them to rise above the challenges that seek to break them down.

Strength is not just a physical attribute but a reservoir of power that lies within the depths of their souls. It is the quiet determination that propels them forward, the unwavering faith in their own worth and abilities. Black women have always been the backbone of their communities, the pillars that uphold our families and shape the future for generations to come. Their strength is a beacon of light in times of darkness, a guiding force that illuminates the path towards a better tomorrow.

In a world that often seeks to erase their voices and diminish their contributions, Black women must stand firm in their power, unapologetically embracing their resilience and strength. They are the embodiment of grace under fire, the fierce warriors who refuse to be silenced.

Their stories are woven into the tapestry of history, a testament to their enduring legacy of resilience and strength.

As we continue to navigate the complexities of a world rife with injustice and inequality, let us draw upon the wellspring of resilience and strength that lies within us. Let us stand together, hand in hand, shoulder to shoulder, as we carve out a path towards a future where Black women are celebrated, uplifted, and empowered to shine brightly as the fierce and formidable forces of nature that they are.

Celebrating Black Womanhood

In this section, we delve into the complexities and nuances that come with being a Black woman, exploring the intersections of race, gender, and identity that shape your experiences. Your journey as a Black woman is one marked by resilience, strength, and a deep-rooted connection to your cultural heritage.

From the legacy of your foremothers who fought for freedom and equality to the constant balancing act of navigating multiple layers of oppression, Black women carry a unique burden that is often overlooked and underestimated. They are both victims of systemic injustices and agents of change, challenging the status quo and advocating for social justice on multiple fronts.

The beauty of Black womanhood lies in their versatility and adaptability, as they move effortlessly between roles as caretakers, activists, professionals, and leaders. They draw inspiration from the strong women who came before them, honoring their legacy while carving out their own paths toward empowerment and liberation.

Their connection to their roots runs deep, grounding them in a sense of belonging and cultural pride that sustains them through adversity. Whether they wear their hair as a crown of glory or speak out against discrimination and inequality, they assert their presence and demand to be seen and heard in a world that too often seeks to silence them.

The bonds of sisterhood among Black women are a source of strength and solidarity, providing a support network that uplifts and empowers them in their journey toward self-discovery and self-actualization. Through shared experiences and shared struggles, they find solace in knowing that they are not alone in their quest for justice, equality, and liberation.

Celebrating Black womanhood is an act of defiance against the forces that seek to diminish their worth and erase their contributions. It is a reaffirmation of their beauty, intelligence, and resilience in the face of adversity, a declaration that they are here, they are powerful, and they will not be silenced.

As Black women, they also navigate the complexities of colorism and internalized oppression. Their varied skin tones are part of a legacy of colonialism and anti-Blackness, with lighter skin often being favored over darker skin in mainstream media and society. This colorism creates divisions within thier own communities, perpetuating harmful stereotypes and beauty standards that devalue the richness and diversity of Black beauty.

Beyond colorism, Black women also face the intersectional challenges of gender and sexuality. LGBTQ+ Black women, in particular, often face additional discrimination and marginalization within both the Black community and the LGBTQ+ community. Their experiences highlight the need for more inclusive and intersectional approaches to advocacy and support for all Black women, regardless of sexual orientation or gender identity.

In the face of these multifaceted challenges, Black women continue to rise and shine, defying expectations and breaking barriers in all areas of society. They excel in entrepreneurship, academia, the arts, and activism, making invaluable contributions to their communities and the world at large. Their voices are powerful, their stories are important, and their presence is essential to creating a more just and equitable society for all.

Thriving in Male-Dominated Spaces

In a society where male-dominated spaces persist, Black women face layered challenges that intersect with their race and gender identities. This intersectionality magnifies the obstacles they encounter, as they navigate environments that reflect deep-seated biases and power dynamics that often marginalize their voices and contributions.

The experiences of Black women in male-dominated spaces are influenced by historical legacies of slavery, colonization, and systemic racism that continue to shape social structures and hierarchies. These historical injustices have perpetuated stereotypes and narratives that cast Black women as less competent, less deserving, or less capable than their male or non-Black counterparts, creating barriers to their advancement and recognition in professional settings.

In addition to facing overt discrimination, Black women often contend with subtler forms of bias, such as microaggressions, tokenism, and the burden of representing their entire race or gender. These experiences can erode their sense of belonging and lead to feelings of isolation and impostor syndrome, as they navigate spaces where their identities are not fully acknowledged or valued.

Despite these challenges, Black women bring a unique perspective and set of strengths to male-dominated environments. Their experiences as double minorities give them a nuanced insight into issues of diversity, equity, and inclusion, allowing them to offer valuable perspectives and solutions that may be overlooked by their peers.

To thrive in male-dominated spaces, Black women must cultivate a strong sense of self-awareness and self-advocacy, recognizing their inherent worth and capabilities. By building networks of support and allies who amplify their voices and champion their success, Black women can create a sense of community and solidarity that bolsters their resilience and empowers them to challenge systems of oppression and discrimination.

Ultimately, thriving in male-dominated spaces as a Black woman requires a steadfast commitment to self-care, self-empowerment, and collective action. By embracing their uniqueness, standing in their truth, and forging paths of resilience and resistance, Black women can not only survive but also thrive in environments that may seek to silence or diminish their presence.

Creating Your Own Path to Success

In a world that often tries to limit them and define their paths according to societal norms and expectations, it is essential for Black women to carve out their own journey to success. This journey may not always be easy, but it is crucial for them to stay true to themselves and follow their dreams with unwavering determination.

Creating their own path to success begins with self-awareness and understanding their unique strengths and passions. Take the time to reflect on what truly matters to you and what you envision for your future. Trust your intuition and have faith in your abilities, even when faced with challenges or setbacks.

It is important to set clear goals for yourself and work towards them with dedication and persistence. Surround yourself with mentors and allies who support and uplift you on your journey. Seek out opportunities for growth and learning, whether through education, networking, or personal development.

As you navigate the challenges and obstacles that may come your way, remember to stay resilient and adaptable. Be open to new possibilities and willing to adjust your plans as needed. Embrace failure as a learning opportunity and use it to fuel your determination to succeed.

Above all, remember that success is not defined by others, but by your own fulfillment and happiness. Stay true to yourself, embrace your individuality, and forge a path that reflects your values and aspirations. By creating your own path to success, you are not only paving the way for yourself but also inspiring future generations of Black women to do the same.

Success for Black women is not just about personal achievement; it is about breaking down barriers and paving the way for others to follow. It is about empowering themselves to be bold, to take risks, and to challenge the status quo. By standing tall in their authenticity and refusing to conform to society's limiting expectations, they set an example for generations to come.

In a world that too often tries to dictate who they should be and what they should aspire to, it is a radical act of self-love and resistance to forge their own paths and define success on their own terms. Do not be bound by the constraints of a society that seeks to confine you; instead break free and soar to heights beyond your wildest dreams.

As a Black woman, your journey to success is a testament to your resilience, strength, and unwavering spirit. It is a manifestation of your ability to overcome adversity and thrive in the face of challenges. Each step you take towards your goals is a defiance of the limitations that society tries to impose on you. It is a declaration of your power and your worth.

In embracing your unique journey to success, you not only uplift yourself but also uplift your communities and pave the way for future generations of Black women to follow. You become a beacon of inspiration, showing what is possible when women dare to dream big and relentlessly pursue their goals. Your success becomes a beacon of hope, a testament to the endless possibilities that exist when women refuse to be confined by the expectations of others.

So continue to walk your own path, proud and unyielding, knowing that in doing so, you are not just shaping your own destiny but also reshaping the world around you. Your success is not just personal triumph; it is a revolution, a transformation, a reclamation of your power and your voice in a world that too often seeks to silence you. Continue to write your own story of success, a story that defies expectations, breaks barriers, and inspires generations to come.

Empowering Future Generations of Black Women

As Black women, it is essential for them to strive towards empowering future generations. Your journey is layered with complexities and challenges, yet your resilience and strength have always been unwavering. In order to empower young Black women coming up behind you, you must continue to pave the way and create opportunities for their success.

Representation plays a crucial role in how young Black women see themselves and their potential. When they see Black women like you breaking barriers, achieving success, and making a difference in the world, it sends a powerful message that their dreams are valid and achievable. It is important for you to continue to be a visible role model, sharing your stories of triumph over adversity and perseverance in the face of obstacles.

Mentorship is a powerful tool that can shape the trajectory of a young Black woman's life. By providing guidance, support, and wisdom, you can help them navigate the complexities of the world and develop the necessary skills to thrive. Through mentorship, you can instill confidence, resilience, and a sense of purpose in the next generation of Black women leaders.

Advocating for systemic change is essential for creating a more equitable and inclusive society for young Black women. By addressing issues of inequality, discrimination, and systemic barriers, you can pave the way for future generations to succeed on a level playing field. It is your duty to challenge the status quo, push for policies that uplift marginalized communities, and create a society where all Black women have the opportunity to reach their full potential.

Intersectionality is a critical lens through which you must view the experiences of Black women. Your identities as a Black woman are multifaceted, and you must acknowledge and address the unique challenges that come with intersecting oppressions. By understanding the nuances of how race, gender, and class intersect in shaping your experiences, you can better support and empower young Black women from all walks of life.

In empowering future generations of Black women, you are not only securing a brighter future for them but also continuing the legacy of resilience, strength, and excellence that has defined Black women throughout history. By investing in their potential, advocating for change, and leading by example, you can ensure that the next generation of Black women are equipped to overcome any obstacle and achieve their greatest dreams.

A strong woman doesn't need anyone's approval. She accepts both compliments and criticism with equal grace and goes after what she wants with passion. She looks a challenge dead in the eye and gives it a wink. She is never afraid to tell it like it is. She knows that strong women need to stick together and build each other up. She is individual and will never require validation from anyone. She loves, forgives, and let's go, and perseveres no matter what life throws at her. She is an empowered woman, strong, self-aware, and a warrior at heart.
— Author unknown

CHAPTER 2

Shattering Black Women Stereotypes

Unveiling the Myths

Deep within the fabric of society lies a web of myths and misconceptions that have shrouded the experiences and identities of Black women for far too long. These myths have been perpetuated through history, media, and cultural narratives, distorting our understanding of Black womanhood and perpetuating harmful stereotypes.

One of the most pervasive myths surrounding Black women is the idea that they are monolithic - that they all fit into a single mold and share the same experiences, perspectives, and struggles. This erases the diversity and complexity of Black women's lives, reducing them to a simplistic caricature that fails to capture the richness of their identities.

Another myth that plagues Black women is the myth of the "Strong Black Woman." While resilience and strength are certainly central to their narratives, the expectation that they must be perpetually strong, self-sacrificing, and unyielding can be detrimental to their well-being. This myth denies them the space to be vulnerable, to seek help when needed, and to prioritize their own mental and emotional well-being.

Additionally, Black women have long been subjected to the myth of hypersexuality, portrayed as lustful and promiscuous beings whose bodies are meant for consumption and objectification. This dehumanizing myth reduces them to mere sexual objects, erasing their agency, autonomy, and humanity.

As we begin to unravel these myths and challenge the narratives that seek to define them, it is crucial to center the voices and experiences of Black women themselves. By embracing their complexities, celebrating their diversity, and affirming their humanity, we can work towards a more inclusive and equitable society that honors the full spectrum of Black womanhood.

In dissecting the myth of the monolithic Black woman, it is important to recognize the vast array of backgrounds, experiences, and perspectives that exist within the Black female community. Black women come from diverse cultural, socioeconomic, and geographic backgrounds, each with their own unique stories and struggles. The misconception that all Black women share the same experiences not only erases this diversity but also undermines the individuality and agency of each woman.

Furthermore, the myth of the "Strong Black Woman" not only places unrealistic expectations on Black women but also overlooks the deep emotional and psychological toll that systemic racism and sexism can take. The pressure to constantly appear strong and resilient can lead to the neglect of mental health and emotional well-being, as Black women may feel compelled to suppress their vulnerabilities and struggles in order to fulfill societal expectations.

Similarly, the hypersexualization of Black women perpetuates harmful stereotypes that dehumanize and objectify them, reducing their identities to mere sexual commodities. This myth not only affects how Black women are perceived and treated in society but also impacts their own self-worth and self-image, as they may internalize these harmful narratives and struggle to assert their agency and autonomy over their bodies and sexuality.

By challenging these myths and narratives, by amplifying the voices and stories of Black women, we can begin to dismantle the harmful stereotypes that have long plagued them. Through centering their own experiences, advocating for their own humanity, and resisting the limitations that society seeks to impose on them, we can forge a path towards a more just and equitable future for all Black women.

Celebrating Black Womanhood

In a world that often seeks to marginalize and overlook them, black women stand as pillars of strength and resilience, their stories woven into the fabric of history. Their journey is one of triumph over adversity, of perseverance in the face of discrimination, and of unwavering determination to be seen and heard.

Black womanhood is a celebration of resilience, beauty, and power. It is a testament to the richness of their experiences, the depth of their emotions, and the breadth of their contributions to society. From Harriet Tubman guiding slaves to freedom on the Underground Railroad to Rosa Parks igniting the Civil Rights Movement with a single act of defiance, black women have been at the forefront of social change, leading with grace and courage.

Their voices, too often silenced or dismissed, ring loud and clear through the annals of history. From the poetry of Maya Angelou to the music of Nina Simone, from the activism of Angela Davis to the leadership of Shirley Chisholm, black women have left an indelible mark on culture, politics, and society.

Celebrating black womanhood is about honoring the strength and resilience that has allowed them to overcome centuries of oppression and injustice. It is about recognizing the beauty and diversity that exists within the black female experience, from the struggles of everyday life to the joys of sisterhood and solidarity.

Black women have not only been trailblazers in the fight for civil rights but have also made significant contributions in fields such as literature, science, business, and the arts. Figures like Zora Neale Hurston, the Harlem Renaissance writer who captured the essence of African American culture in her works, or Mae Jemison, the first African American woman astronaut who shattered barriers in space exploration, exemplify the diverse talents and achievements of black women.

Moreover, black women play essential roles in their communities as mothers, caregivers, activists, and leaders. Their resilience and ability to overcome adversity inspire others to persevere in the face of challenges. Whether advocating for social justice, promoting education and economic empowerment, or simply being a source of strength and support for their families and communities, black women continue to shape the world around them with their unwavering spirit and determination.

In addition to their individual accomplishments, black women have also been instrumental in shaping cultural movements and political progress. From the civil rights era to the modern-day Black Lives Matter movement, black women have been at the forefront of advocating for equality, justice, and representation. Figures like Fannie Lou Hamer, Audre Lorde, and Bell Hooks have used their voices to challenge systems of oppression and uplift marginalized voices.

The intersectionality of race and gender adds another layer of complexity to the experiences of black women. Not only have they had to navigate systemic racism, but they have also faced sexism and misogyny within their communities and society at large. Despite these intersecting challenges, black women have continued to rise and fight for their rights and the rights of others, embodying strength and resilience in the face of adversity.

Overall, celebrating black womanhood is about recognizing the multifaceted identities, experiences, and contributions of black women throughout history and in the present day. Their stories are not just stories of struggle but also of triumph, joy, love, and sisterhood. Black women continue to inspire and empower generations to come, their legacy of strength and resilience paving the way for a more just and equitable future for all.

Resilience in the Face of Adversity

In the face of adversity, Black women have displayed an unmatched strength and resilience that has inspired generations. Time and time again, they have faced hardships and challenges with unwavering determination and grace.

From the days of slavery to the civil rights movement to present-day struggles for equality, Black women have stood at the forefront of the fight for justice. Their resilience in the face of systemic racism, sexism, and discrimination serves as a powerful example of endurance and perseverance.

Black women have not only faced external adversities but also internal struggles within their own communities. They have often been marginalized and overlooked, fighting not only against external forces but also against stereotypes and prejudices from within their own communities.

Despite these intersecting challenges, Black women have continued to rise above adversity, breaking down barriers and shattering glass ceilings along the way. Their resilience is a testament to the power of the human spirit and the belief that change is possible, even in the darkest of times.

Through their resilience, Black women have shown the world what it means to be strong, courageous, and unyielding in the face of adversity.

Their stories serve as a beacon of hope and inspiration for all who face challenges in their own lives, reminding us that we, too, can overcome anything with determination and resilience.

It is through their collective strength and unwavering resilience that Black women have been able to create lasting change and pave the way for future generations. Their impact extends far beyond their individual experiences, leaving a legacy of resilience and empowerment that will continue to inspire and uplift for years to come.

The resilience of Black women is deeply rooted in their history of overcoming adversity and oppression. Starting from the days of slavery, Black women were subjected to unimaginable cruelty and dehumanization, yet they found ways to survive and resist. Whether it was through acts of quiet defiance or bold resistance, Black women refused to let their spirits be broken.

During the civil rights movement, Black women played crucial roles in organizing protests, leading marches, and advocating for change. Women like Rosa Parks, Ella Baker, and Fannie Lou Hamer stood as fierce pillars of strength, challenging the status quo and demanding justice for themselves and their communities.

In the present day, Black women continue to face systemic challenges that threaten their well-being and livelihoods. From disparities in healthcare to wage gaps in the workforce, Black women navigate a society that often overlooks their voices and struggles. Yet, despite these obstacles, they persist with resilience and determination, refusing to be silenced or sidelined.

The resilience of Black women is not just a personal attribute but a cultural and historical phenomenon. It is a legacy passed down through generations, a strength born out of necessity and nurtured through shared experiences. Black women draw upon this wellspring of resilience to navigate the complexities of being both Black and female in a world that seeks to diminish their worth and potential.

Through their resilience, Black women have created spaces for healing, empowerment, and collective action. They have formed networks of support and solidarity, amplifying each other's voices and standing together in the face of adversity. Their resilience is a source of inspiration for all who witness their strength and grace in the midst of adversity, a reminder that the human spirit can triumph over even the most daunting challenges.

Challenging Societal Expectations

As a Black woman in today's society, the layers of expectations that encase them run deep, intertwining with the threads of history, culture, and identity that have shaped their existence. From the moment they open their eyes to the world each day, they navigate a landscape peppered with societal norms and stereotypes that seek to confine them within confines not of their choosing.

The weight of these expectations, often invisible to those who do not bear them, can feel like a heavy cloak draped over their shoulders, dictating their every move and stifling the essence of who they truly are. The world expects them to be strong, resilient, and unwavering in the face of adversity, but often forgets that these qualities do not preclude vulnerability, tenderness, or moments of doubt.

The dichotomies of expectation compound, demanding that they embody confidence without being perceived as arrogant, assertiveness without being labeled aggressive, success without evoking fear or jealousy. It is a tightrope walk between authenticity and conformity, between self-preservation and societal acceptance.

Yet, within the midst of these contradictions, they find their voices - a voice that speaks truths borne from generations of resilience, struggle, and triumph. It is a voice that refuses to be dimmed, a beacon of light that illuminates the shadows of oppression and inequality. It is a voice that carries the echoes of their ancestors, their hardships, their victories, their enduring spirit.

In reclaiming and amplifying this voice, they stand not only for themselves but for all Black women who have been silenced and marginalized throughout history. I stand in solidarity with those who have been systematically denied their humanity, their dignity, and their right to exist freely in a world that seeks to confine them to the margins.

Black women draw strength from the tapestry of their heritage, weaving threads of resilience, creativity, and joy into the fabric of their existence. I honor the struggles of my foremothers, the sacrifices they made, the battles they fought, the victories they won. Their legacy fuels their determination to break the chains of expectation and carve out a space where authenticity, intersectionality, and empowerment reign supreme.

Black women refuse to be a mere footnote in someone else's narrative, a token of diversity or a mirage of progress. They are a force to be reckoned with, a wellspring of wisdom and power that transcends the limitations imposed upon them. Therefore, Black women are unapologetically, a living testament to the beauty, strength, and resilience of the community.

Defying Stereotypes - The Strength Within

In a world fraught with historical injustices and systemic inequalities, Black women have endured a unique and often overlooked struggle for recognition and empowerment. Through the centuries, they have faced a myriad of challenges, from slavery and segregation to discrimination and marginalization. Despite these adversities, Black women have consistently demonstrated a profound resilience and inner strength that transcends the limitations imposed upon them by society.

The strength of Black women is rooted in their ancestral legacy of survival and resistance. From the bonds of sisterhood forged during the days of slavery to the grassroots movements for civil rights and gender equality in more recent times, Black women have always been at the forefront of social change. Their voices, though often marginalized, have carried the weight of generations of silenced stories and struggles.

One cannot fully grasp the depth of Black women's strength without acknowledging the intersectionality of their identities. Black women navigate a complex web of race, gender, and class, each layer informing their experiences and shaping their perspectives. Their strength lies not only in their ability to overcome individual challenges but also in their capacity to uplift and support their communities as a whole.

The resilience of Black women is a testament to their unwavering belief in justice and equity. Time and time again, they have stood up against injustice, fought for their rights, and championed the cause of equality for all. Their courage in the face of adversity serves as a beacon of hope and inspiration for those around them, igniting a spark of change that ripples through society.

As Black women continue to push boundaries and break down barriers, their strength and resilience serve as a powerful reminder of the indomitable human spirit. They embody a legacy of courage and determination that transcends time and place, offering a vision of possibility and empowerment for future generations. In every step they take, every word they speak, and every barrier they defy, Black women redefine what it means to be strong, resilient, and unapologetically themselves.

The power of Black women's strength extends beyond their individual experiences and resonates on a collective level. Their resilience is not just a personal attribute but a communal force that binds communities together and propels movements forward. Through their leadership, creativity, and unwavering commitment to change, Black women inspire others to rise up and make their voices heard.

Furthermore, the strength of Black women is not limited to their struggles but also encompasses their joy, resilience, and capacity for love. In the face of adversity, Black women have found solace in their communities, their art, and their culture. They have embraced their heritage, celebrated their identities, and reclaimed their narratives in a world that often seeks to silence them.

In essence, the strength of Black women transcends boundaries, defies expectations, and challenges the status quo. It is a force that radiates from within, fueled by a deep sense of purpose and a commitment to justice. As Black women continue to navigate the complexities of their experiences and advocate for a more equitable world, their strength serves as a beacon of hope and a testament to the resilience of the human spirit.

Pioneers of Progress

In this section, we delve into the stories of remarkable Black women who have blazed trails and broken barriers in various fields. From the brave activists who fought for civil rights to the pioneering scientists who revolutionized their fields, these women inspire us with their courage, passion, and unwavering determination. Their stories serve as a testament to the power of resilience and the impact of persistent dedication. By highlighting their achievements, we not only celebrate their successes but also shed light on the challenges they faced and overcame.

One such inspirational figure is Rosa Parks, known as the "mother of the civil rights movement." Her refusal to give up her seat on a segregated bus in Montgomery, Alabama in 1955 sparked the Montgomery Bus Boycott and brought international attention to the injustices of segregation. Despite facing backlash and threats, Parks remained steadfast in her commitment to justice and equality.

In the realm of science, we see the contributions of Mae Jemison, the first African American woman to travel to space. Jemison, a physician and astronaut, shattered barriers with her historic journey aboard the Space Shuttle Endeavour in 1992. Her achievements paved the way for future generations of women and minorities to pursue careers in STEM fields.

Furthermore, we cannot overlook the groundbreaking work of Shirley Chisholm, the first Black woman elected to the United States Congress and the first Black candidate for a major party's nomination for President of the United States. Chisholm's fearless advocacy for marginalized communities and her unapologetic stance on issues of social justice continue to inspire activists and politicians today.

These pioneers of progress remind us that change is possible, that dreams can be realized, and that the journey to equality and empowerment is ongoing. Their legacies continue to shape our world and challenge us to strive for a more just and inclusive society.

Expanding our exploration, we also see the extraordinary achievements of other Black women such as Octavia E. Butler, a pioneering science fiction writer known for her imaginative and thought-provoking works. Butler's novels, including "Kindred" and the "Parable" series, explore themes of race, gender, and power, pushing the boundaries of the genre and inspiring readers with her visionary storytelling.

Additionally, we must recognize the impactful contributions of Fannie Lou Hamer, a fierce advocate for voting rights and civil rights. Hamer, a sharecropper from Mississippi, co-founded the Mississippi Freedom Democratic Party and bravely stood up to discrimination and violence in her quest for equality. Her powerful speeches and organizing efforts were instrumental in bringing attention to the struggles of Black Americans in the segregated South.

Furthermore, we look to the accomplishments of influential figures like Toni Morrison, the Nobel Prize-winning author whose works, such as "Beloved" and "Song of Solomon," have profoundly influenced literature and challenged readers to confront the complexities of race, identity, and history in America. Morrison's powerful storytelling and lyrical prose have earned her a place among the greatest literary voices of our time.

As we reflect on the lives and legacies of these remarkable Black women, we are reminded of the indelible mark they have left on history and the enduring impact of their courage, resilience, and unwavering commitment to justice and equality. Their stories serve as an inspiration to us all, urging us to continue the work of building a more inclusive and equitable world for future generations.

Breaking Barriers in the Workplace

In a world where biases and stereotypes still prevail, Black women have had to navigate countless barriers in the workplace. From microaggressions to systemic discrimination, their journey has been anything but easy. Despite these challenges, Black women have risen above adversity and shattered glass ceilings in various industries.

The workplace is often seen as a battlefield where Black women must constantly prove their worth and competence. Many face the double burden of racism and sexism, dealing with stereotypes that undermine their abilities and potential. However, instead of succumbing to these obstacles, Black women have chosen to challenge the status quo and demand their rightful place at the table.

Through resilience, determination, and unwavering courage, Black women have become trailblazers in the corporate world, entrepreneurship, academia, and beyond. They have demonstrated exceptional leadership skills, innovative thinking, and a unique perspective that enriches organizations and drives positive change.

Despite facing institutional barriers and unequal opportunities, Black women continue to break new ground and pave the way for future generations. Their success serves as a beacon of hope and inspiration for all who dare to dream big and defy societal limitations.

By breaking barriers in the workplace, Black women are not only advancing their own careers but also dismantling oppressive structures that have long hindered their progress. Their presence and achievements challenge outdated norms and push for greater diversity, equity, and inclusion in all spheres of society.

The journey towards workplace equality is far from over, but with the resilience and tenacity of Black women leading the way, there is hope for a future where talent and merit are the only measures of success. Together, we can break down barriers and create a more inclusive and equitable world for all.

Black women have also excelled in fields such as technology, science, arts, and social justice activism, showcasing their diverse talents and contributions to society. They have pioneered groundbreaking research, created innovative products, and spearheaded movements for social change. Through their work and advocacy, Black women have challenged dominant narratives and inspired others to pursue their passions fearlessly.

Moreover, the intersectionality of being both Black and female has shaped the experiences and struggles of Black women in unique ways. They often face compounded discrimination and marginalization, navigating complex identity dynamics while striving for success and recognition. Despite these challenges, Black women have embraced their intersectional identities with pride and resilience, using their voices to amplify marginalized perspectives and advocate for justice and equality.

As we celebrate the achievements of Black women in the workplace and beyond, it is crucial to acknowledge the structural barriers and historical injustices that continue to hinder their progress. Systemic racism, sexism, and economic disparities pose significant challenges for

Black women, limiting their opportunities for advancement and representation. It is imperative for organizations and society as a whole to address these inequalities and create inclusive environments where Black women can thrive and excel without fear of discrimination or bias.

In elevating the voices and experiences of Black women, we not only honor their resilience and contributions but also recognize the urgent need for systemic change to ensure equity and justice for all. The journey towards true equality requires collective action, solidarity, and a commitment to dismantling oppressive systems that perpetuate inequality. By centering the experiences of Black women and valuing their leadership and expertise, we can create a more just and inclusive society where every individual has the opportunity to succeed and thrive.

Embracing Authenticity

Embracing authenticity is a profound journey of self-discovery and self-acceptance that transcends societal norms and expectations. It is a transformative process that requires introspection, courage, and a willingness to let go of the masks they wear to please others.

At its core, embracing authenticity is an act of reclaiming your true self from the conditioning and external influences that may have shaped you. It involves peeling back the layers of societal expectations, past traumas, and self-doubt to uncover the essence of who you are at your core. This process can be both liberating and challenging, as it requires you to confront your fears and vulnerabilities with compassion and self-compassion.

When you embrace authenticity, you are honoring the unique gifts, talents, and quirks that make you who you are. You celebrate your individuality and reject the idea that you need to conform to fit in or be accepted. By embracing your authentic self, you empower others to do the same, creating a ripple effect of self-love and acceptance in our communities and beyond.

Living authentically also means being in alignment with your values and beliefs, even when it means standing alone or facing criticism. It requires you to be courageous in expressing your truths and setting boundaries that honor your authenticity. When you are true to yourself, you attract people and opportunities that align with your highest good, leading to greater fulfillment and genuine connections.

Embracing authenticity is not about striving for perfection or seeking external validation. It is about embracing your imperfections and vulnerabilities as integral parts of who you are. By embracing your authentic self, you cultivate a deep sense of self-worth and inner peace that emanates outward, inspiring others to do the same.

In a world that often values conformity and sameness, choosing to embrace authenticity is a revolutionary act of self-love and self-empowerment. It is a journey that leads you back to yourself, where you find the courage and strength to live in alignment with your truest self, unapologetically and authentically.

Ultimately, embracing authenticity is a lifelong practice that requires ongoing self-awareness and self-compassion. It allows you to live with integrity and depth, navigating the complexities of life with grace and resilience. By embracing your authentic self, you unlock the power of your innermost being and pave the way for genuine connections, meaningful contributions, and a life filled with purpose and fulfillment.

Cultivating Self-Worth

Self-worth is a fundamental aspect of our human experience, shaping our thoughts, emotions, and behaviors in profound ways. It is the foundation upon which our sense of identity, value, and belonging are built, influencing every decision we make and every interaction we have. Yet, despite its significance, self-worth is often elusive, subject to the ebb and flow of external validation, societal standards, and internalized beliefs.

To truly cultivate self-worth, we must embark on a journey of self-exploration that goes beyond surface-level assessments and dives deep into the core of our being. This journey begins with self-awareness, a practice of tuning into our thoughts, emotions, and reactions with curiosity and compassion. By examining the patterns of self-talk, self-criticism, and self-doubt that reverberate within us, we can uncover the roots of our self-worth issues and begin to untangle the web of conditioning that has shaped our sense of worth.

Self-compassion is a key ingredient in the process of cultivating self-worth. It involves treating ourselves with the same kindness, understanding, and acceptance that we would offer to a dear friend in times of struggle or pain. By embracing our imperfections, failures, and vulnerabilities with a sense of gentleness and grace, we shift from a mindset of self-judgment to one of self-love. This shift in perspective allows us to see ourselves through a lens of empathy and warmth, fostering a deep sense of worthiness and belonging.

Setting boundaries is a powerful practice that reinforces our sense of self-worth and self-respect. Boundaries serve as a protective shield, safeguarding our emotional, physical, and mental well-being from external threats and intrusions. By clearly defining what is acceptable and what is not in our relationships, work environments, and personal lives, we establish a sense of agency and autonomy that affirms our worth and value. Boundaries serve as a tangible expression of self-care and self-respect, signaling to ourselves and others that our needs and limits are deserving of respect.

Self-care practices play a vital role in nurturing and sustaining our self-worth. Engaging in activities that replenish our spirit, nourish our body, and soothe our mind is a tangible expression of self-love and self-compassion. Whether it be practicing mindfulness, engaging in creative pursuits, or spending time in nature, self-care rituals provide a sanctuary of self-nourishment and rejuvenation. By prioritizing our well-being and investing in activities that bring us joy and fulfillment, we reaffirm our intrinsic worth and value.

Challenging limiting beliefs and negative self-talk is a crucial step in expanding our self-worth. These internalized messages, often rooted in past experiences or societal conditioning, can erode our self-esteem and undermine our sense of self-worth. By developing a practice of cognitive restructuring and self-reflection, we can identify and challenge these harmful beliefs, replacing them with empowering and affirming thoughts. This process of inner work is transformative, opening the door to a renewed sense of self-worth and self-empowerment.

In conclusion, cultivating self-worth is a profound journey of self-discovery, self-acceptance, and self-empowerment. It requires a commitment to inner exploration, self-compassion, boundary-setting, self-care, and belief restructuring. By embracing our authentic selves, honoring our needs and boundaries, and cultivating a mindset of self-respect and self-love, we can unlock the depths of our inherent worth and embrace a life of fulfillment, authenticity, and empowerment.

Empowering Future Generations

In this section, we delve into the crucial role that empowering future generations plays in creating a more equitable and inclusive society. We explore the various ways in which we can uplift and support young individuals, particularly those from marginalized communities, to help them reach their full potential.

Through mentorship, education, and advocacy, we can instill the values of self-worth and resilience in the next generation. By providing them with the tools and opportunities to thrive, we can break the cycle of oppression and create a brighter future for all.

It is essential to acknowledge the systemic barriers that exist for many young people, particularly those from marginalized backgrounds. Structural inequalities, such as lack of access to quality education, healthcare, and economic opportunities, can hinder their ability to succeed. By addressing these disparities and advocating for policies that promote equity and social justice, we can create a more level playing field for all youth.

Representation and visibility are also key pillars of empowering future generations. When young people see individuals who look like them in positions of influence and success, it inspires them to dream big and aspire to achieve greatness. Diversity in leadership and media representation is crucial in shaping the aspirations and self-perception of young individuals, reinforcing the message that their voices matter and their potential is unlimited.

Furthermore, fostering a sense of community and belonging is essential in empowering future generations. Providing safe spaces for young people to express themselves, share their experiences, and support one another can bolster their confidence and resilience. Strong social networks and mentorship programs can offer guidance and encouragement, helping young individuals navigate challenges and pursue their goals with determination.

Moreover, investing in the mental health and emotional well-being of young people is critical in empowering them to succeed. The pressures of today's society can take a toll on the mental health of youth, leading to increased stress, anxiety, and depression. By providing access to mental health resources, counseling services, and promoting a culture of well-being, we can support young individuals in coping with challenges and developing healthy coping mechanisms.

Additionally, cultivating an understanding of intersectionality is essential in empowering future generations. Recognizing the interconnected nature of social identities, such as race, gender, sexuality, and socioeconomic status, can help us address the unique challenges and barriers faced by marginalized youth. By taking an intersectional approach to empowerment, we can ensure that all young individuals receive the support and advocacy they need to thrive.

In conclusion, empowering future generations is an ongoing process that requires collective action, empathy, and commitment. By investing in the potential of young people and creating a nurturing environment that fosters growth and resilience, we can build a more inclusive and equitable society for generations to come.

"Turn your wounds into wisdom"
— Oprah Winfrey

CHAPTER 3

Healing

Reclaiming Vulnerability: Embracing Your Emotions

In a world that often tells us to hide our emotions, to toughen up, and to push through, the idea of reclaiming vulnerability can feel daunting. Yet, true strength lies in our ability to embrace our emotions, to allow ourselves to feel deeply and authentically.

Vulnerability is not weakness; it is courage. It takes courage to be open and honest with ourselves and others about how we truly feel. By embracing our emotions, we acknowledge our humanity and connect more deeply with our inner selves.

When we suppress or ignore our emotions, we can create a barrier between ourselves and others. We may struggle to form genuine connections and build meaningful relationships. But when we allow ourselves to be vulnerable, we invite others to see us for who we truly are, flaws and all.

Embracing our emotions also allows us to process and release what we are feeling. By acknowledging and expressing our emotions, we give ourselves the opportunity to heal and grow. Whether we are experiencing joy, sadness, anger, fear, or any other emotion, allowing ourselves to feel without judgment is a powerful act of self-love.

This act of vulnerability can lead to profound personal growth and self-discovery. When we allow ourselves to be open and raw, we create space for authenticity and genuine connections to blossom. By sharing our vulnerabilities with others, we build trust and deepen our relationships, fostering a sense of community and acceptance.

Furthermore, embracing vulnerability can also lead to increased resilience. When we confront our emotions head-on, we learn to navigate life's challenges with grace and courage. Rather than being weighed down by our emotions, we learn to embrace them as a natural part of the human experience, strengthening our emotional fortitude and empowering us to face whatever comes our way.

In essence, reclaiming vulnerability is an act of reclaiming our humanity. It is a testament to our courage, our strength, and our capacity for growth. By allowing ourselves to be vulnerable, we open ourselves up to profound personal transformation, deeper connections with others, and a more authentic and fulfilling life.

Embracing vulnerability requires us to practice self-compassion and self-awareness. It means being willing to sit with discomfort, to face our fears, and to lean into our emotions with curiosity and kindness. This process of self-exploration can be both challenging and liberating, as we uncover layers of ourselves that have long been buried beneath the facade of strength and invulnerability.

As we journey inward and embrace our vulnerabilities, we not only cultivate greater empathy and understanding for ourselves but also for others. We learn to see the beauty in imperfection, the strength in vulnerability, and the power in authenticity. Our capacity for connection deepens, our relationships become more authentic, and our sense of self-worth blossoms.

In a society that often equates vulnerability with weakness, choosing to embrace our emotions and share our truths requires a radical shift in mindset. It is a courageous act of rebellion against conformity and a bold declaration of self-acceptance. When we dare to be vulnerable, we defy societal norms that demand perfection and invincibility, and we pave the way for a more compassionate and empathetic world.

The Myth of the Strong Black Woman

The myth of the Strong Black Woman is a complex and deeply ingrained stereotype that has had lasting implications on the lives of Black women in America. Stemming from a long history of resilience and survival in the face of oppression, the archetype of the Strong Black Woman has become a double-edged sword for Black women, shaping both external perceptions and internal expectations.

Rooted in the legacy of slavery, where Black women were forced to endure inhumane conditions and labor without reprieve, the myth of the Strong Black Woman emerged as a means of survival. Black women were expected to bear the brunt of physical labor, emotional trauma, and sexual exploitation, all while maintaining a facade of strength and fortitude. This historical legacy has translated into modern-day expectations for Black women to be unyielding, unwavering pillars of strength in the face of adversity.

The myth of the Strong Black Woman is not simply a reflection of the resilience and strength inherent in Black women, but also a product of systems of oppression that seek to pigeonhole and dehumanize them. The stereotype often erases the complexities of Black women's experiences, denying them the space to be vulnerable, imperfect, or in need of support. This perpetuation of the Strong Black Woman myth can have damaging effects on mental health, relationships, and overall well-being, as Black women may internalize the pressure to constantly perform strength at the expense of their own needs and boundaries.

Intersectionality plays a significant role in shaping the experiences of Black women within the confines of the Strong Black Woman myth. Black women who also identify as LGBTQ+, disabled, immigrant, or belonging to other marginalized groups may face compounded challenges in navigating societal expectations of strength and resilience. The intersection of race, gender, and other identities further complicates the notion of strength and underscores the importance of recognizing the diverse experiences and needs of Black women.

In order to challenge and dismantle the myth of the Strong Black Woman, it is essential to acknowledge the harmful effects of this stereotype and work towards creating spaces that affirm and celebrate the multifaceted nature of Black women's experiences. By rejecting unrealistic standards of strength and embracing vulnerability, Black women can redefine their narratives on their own terms, honoring their resilience while also prioritizing their well-being and self-care. Breaking free from the confines of the Strong Black Woman myth is a radical act of self-love and liberation, a step towards empowerment and authenticity in a world that often seeks to diminish the humanity and agency of Black women.

Unpacking Childhood Trauma

Childhood trauma is a complex and multifaceted phenomenon that can have far-reaching effects on an individual's emotional, psychological, and physical well-being. The experiences of our formative years, especially those marked by adversity, can leave lasting imprints on our minds and bodies, shaping the way we perceive ourselves, others, and the world around us.

The impact of childhood trauma is not limited to the immediate aftermath of a distressing event; rather, it can manifest in various ways throughout an individual's life, influencing their beliefs, behaviors, and relationships. For some, the scars of childhood trauma may remain hidden beneath a façade of strength and resilience, while for others, they may surface in the form of anxiety, depression, or other mental health challenges.

One of the defining characteristics of childhood trauma is its disruptive effect on the developing brain and nervous system. When a child is exposed to prolonged stress or adversity, their brain may adapt in ways that prioritize survival over long-term well-being, leading to alterations in neural pathways and responses to stress. This can result in a heightened state of hyperarousal or hypervigilance, making it difficult for individuals to relax, trust others, or feel safe in their environment.

Moreover, the emotional toll of childhood trauma can be equally profound, often manifesting in symptoms such as flashbacks, nightmares, and intrusive memories. The emotional pain of unprocessed trauma may linger beneath the surface, impacting an individual's self-esteem, sense of identity, and ability to form healthy attachments with others. It can create a pervasive sense of shame, self-blame, or unworthiness that colors their perceptions of themselves and their place in the world.

In navigating the aftermath of childhood trauma, individuals may find themselves grappling with a range of complex emotions, from anger and grief to fear and numbness. The journey of healing from childhood trauma requires courage, patience, and a willingness to confront the pain and discomfort that arises along the way. It involves creating a safe space within oneself to explore and process difficult memories, emotions, and beliefs, with the support of trusted individuals and therapeutic interventions.

Through this process of self-exploration and healing, individuals can begin to reclaim their sense of agency, autonomy, and self-worth. They can learn to cultivate self-compassion, build resilience, and develop healthy coping strategies to navigate the challenges of life with greater ease and authenticity. By acknowledging and honoring the impact of childhood trauma on their lives, individuals can pave the way for profound growth, healing, and ultimately, a renewed sense of wholeness and well-being.

Healing Starts Within: Cultivating Self-Compassion

In delving further into the multifaceted realm of nurturing self-compassion and internal healing, we embark on a profound exploration of the intricate layers that compose the essential fabric of self-acceptance and understanding. This enlightening journey requires a fundamental shift in consciousness, where the realization dawns that self-compassion is not a mere act of kindness towards oneself but an intrinsic source of inner strength and resilience.

At the core of cultivating self-compassion lies the recognition of our interconnectedness with the universal human experience. By acknowledging that suffering and pain are shared elements of the human condition, we can transcend the barriers of self-isolation and embrace a compassionate attitude towards ourselves and others. This perspective enables us to release the grip of self-criticism and comparison, allowing us to hold our imperfections and vulnerabilities with a gentle, nurturing touch.

Moreover, the practice of self-compassion entails the cultivation of mindfulness and self-awareness as essential pillars of inner growth. Through the lens of mindfulness, we learn to observe our thoughts and emotions without judgment, cultivating a sense of inner space and clarity. This mindful awareness empowers us to recognize our patterns of self-criticism and negative self-talk, paving the way for compassionate intervention and transformation.

In addition to mindfulness, embracing self-care practices becomes a vital component of the journey towards self-compassion. Engaging in activities that nourish our body, mind, and spirit, such as exercise, meditation, or creative expression, reinforces our commitment to self-nurturance and well-being. By prioritizing self-care, we signal to ourselves and the world our inherent worthiness and value, fostering a deep sense of self-love and respect.

As we continue to navigate the intricate path of self-compassion, we uncover the profound layers of our inner landscape, unveiling hidden reservoirs of strength, resilience, and wisdom. Through the transformative power of self-compassion, we embark on a journey of healing and self-discovery, paving the way for a profound sense of inner peace, authenticity, and empowerment. Embracing self-compassion as a guiding principle in our lives, we unleash the boundless potential for growth and transformation that resides within each of us, illuminating our path towards wholeness and self-fulfillment.

Setting Boundaries: Protecting Your Emotional Wellbeing

In addition to protecting your emotional wellbeing, setting boundaries is also crucial for maintaining a sense of self and fostering healthy self-esteem. When we establish and maintain boundaries, we are declaring to ourselves and others that our needs and values are important and deserving of respect. This affirmation of self-worth is essential for cultivating a strong sense of identity and self-assurance.

By setting boundaries, we create a framework that allows us to navigate the complexities of relationships with clarity and integrity. Boundaries serve as a guide for how we expect to be treated and provide a structure for healthy communication and interaction. When our boundaries are respected, we feel validated and understood, strengthening our sense of self and deepening our connections with others.

Furthermore, setting boundaries can help prevent burnout and feelings of resentment. When we consistently prioritize others' needs over our own and fail to establish boundaries, we risk sacrificing our own well-being in the process. By clearly defining our limits and honoring our own needs, we create a more sustainable balance in our relationships and avoid feelings of overwhelm and exhaustion.

It's important to recognize that setting boundaries is a skill that requires practice and self-awareness. It may feel uncomfortable or challenging at first, especially if you are accustomed to putting others' needs before your own. However, with time and persistence, you can become more confident in asserting your boundaries and advocating for your emotional wellbeing.

In our interconnected world, where technology often blurs the lines between work and personal life, setting boundaries becomes even more essential. Establishing clear limits around when and how we engage with technology can help protect our mental and emotional health, ensuring that we have time for rest, relaxation, and meaningful connections with loved ones.

Moreover, setting boundaries is not about building walls or shutting people out; it's about creating healthy parameters that promote mutual respect and understanding. Effective communication is key in setting boundaries, as it allows us to express our needs and expectations clearly, while also listening to the boundaries of others.

In conclusion, setting boundaries is a powerful tool for safeguarding your emotional health, nurturing your sense of self-worth, and promoting healthy relationships. By establishing clear boundaries and communicating them assertively, you empower yourself to create fulfilling connections and live authentically in alignment with your values and needs.

The Impact of Unhealed Trauma on Relationships

In the intricate dance of human relationships, the echoes of unhealed trauma reverberate through the chambers of the heart, shaping the contours of our interactions in subtle yet profound ways. When the tendrils of past pain creep into the present moment, they cast a shadow over our capacity to love and be loved, to trust and be trusted, to truly connect with one another on a soul-deep level.

The impact of unhealed trauma on relationships goes beyond mere surface-level dynamics; it seeps into the very foundation of our emotional landscape, coloring the way we perceive ourselves and others. The wounds we carry, whether from childhood experiences, past relationships, or other sources of pain, act as silent inhibitors, distorting our perceptions and influencing our behaviors in ways we may not fully understand.

At the core of unhealed trauma lies a tangled web of unresolved emotions, unexpressed needs, and deeply ingrained beliefs about ourselves and the world around us. These invisible scars can manifest as a fear of intimacy, a reluctance to show vulnerability, or a tendency to repeat self-destructive patterns that keep us mired in cycles of pain and disconnection.

In relationships, the repercussions of unhealed trauma can be particularly insidious. We may find ourselves caught in a perpetual dance of push and pull, drawing closer to our loved ones only to retreat at the first sign of perceived threat. Our communication may falter, our emotions may run amok, and our ability to forge deep, meaningful connections may be hindered by the walls we inadvertently erect to shield ourselves from further harm.

The struggle to navigate the murky waters of unhealed trauma in relationships is both a personal journey and a shared endeavor. It calls for an unwavering commitment to self-awareness, a willingness to confront the shadows within and without, and a profound sense of empathy for the struggles of our partners as they grapple with their own inner demons.

Healing from unhealed trauma is a transformative process that requires courage, compassion, and a deep-seated belief in the power of human connection to transcend even the darkest of shadows. It demands that we confront our past with open hearts and minds, that we confront our pain with unwavering resolve, and that we confront our fears with the knowledge that true healing can only come from facing the darkness within and allowing it to be transformed by the light of love and understanding.

As we embark on this journey of healing in relationships, we may stumble and falter, we may face setbacks and challenges, but we must never lose sight of the beacon of hope that shines brightly in the depths of our hearts. With each step forward, with each act of courage and vulnerability, we move closer to a place of wholeness, where the scars of our past no longer dictate the shape of our future, and where the bonds we forge with others are forged in the crucible of shared growth and mutual understanding.

The impact of unhealed trauma on relationships is a potent force, but it is not an insurmountable obstacle. It is a call to arms, a summons to embark on a journey of self-discovery and healing that has the power to transform not only our relationships but also our very souls. May we have the strength to heed that call, the courage to face our demons, and the faith to believe that love, in all its forms, has the power to heal even the deepest wounds.

In the tapestry of human connection, the threads of unhealed trauma weave a complex and intricate pattern, shaping the way we relate to others and ourselves. The ghostly whispers of past hurts linger in the spaces between us, coloring our interactions with shades of fear, mistrust, and pain. We may find ourselves entangled in a web of unresolved emotions, repeating old patterns that keep us stuck in cycles of dysfunction and disconnection.

The roots of unhealed trauma run deep, reaching into the very core of our being and shaping the lens through which we view the world. Our experiences of hurt and betrayal, abandonment and loss, leave imprints on our souls that can distort our perceptions, cloud our judgments, and hinder our ability to engage authentically in relationships. The wounds we carry act as invisible barriers, guarding our hearts and preventing us from fully opening up to the possibility of deep connection and intimacy.

In the realm of relationships, the impact of unhealed trauma can manifest in a myriad of ways. We may struggle to communicate effectively, to express our needs and boundaries, or to trust in the goodwill of our partners. We may find ourselves caught in patterns of behavior that perpetuate pain and conflict, unable to break free from the grip of past wounds that continue to haunt us in the present. Our fear of vulnerability and rejection may lead us to build walls around our hearts, keeping others at arm's length and denying ourselves the chance to experience the transformative power of true intimacy.

To navigate the maze of unhealed trauma in relationships is to embark on a journey of self-discovery and healing, a path fraught with challenges and rewards. It requires us to delve deep into the recesses of our psyche, to confront our inner demons with courage and compassion, and to unravel the tangled knots of past pain that bind us to patterns of dysfunction and disconnection. It calls for a willingness to be vulnerable, to face our fears and insecurities head-on, and to cultivate a sense of self-awareness and self-compassion that can guide us through the turbulent waters of healing and growth.

As we embark on this journey of healing in relationships, we must be willing to embrace the discomfort of dismantling our defenses, of peeling back the layers of protection that shield us from the rawness of our emotions and the depths of our pain. We must cultivate a sense of empathy and understanding for ourselves and others, recognizing that we are all wounded beings in need of healing and grace. In the crucible of shared vulnerability and mutual support, we can begin to forge connections that are built on a foundation of trust, respect, and authenticity, transcending the confines of past trauma and opening up new vistas of love and connection.

The path to healing from unhealed trauma in relationships is a challenging and arduous one, requiring us to confront our shadows and fears with unwavering courage and determination. Yet, in the crucible of transformation, we can emerge stronger, wiser, and more whole, ready to embrace the fullness of life and love that awaits us on the other side of healing. May we embark on this journey with open hearts and minds, trusting in the power of love to guide us through the darkness and into the light of healing and growth.

Breaking the Cycle: Healing Generational Trauma

In order to break the cycle of generational trauma, we must first acknowledge and understand the profound impact it has on our lives. Generational trauma is the enduring legacy of pain and suffering passed down through the ages, lingering like a dark shadow over our families and shaping our very identities. It is the silent whispers of ancestors' unvoiced sorrows and unhealed wounds that echo through the corridors of time, influencing our thoughts, beliefs, and behaviors in ways we may not even fully comprehend.

The transmission of generational trauma is a complex and multifaceted process, often weaving through the fabric of our familial relationships and shaping the very foundation of who we are. From the scars of war and persecution to the wounds of slavery and colonization, the traumas of our ancestors have left an indelible mark on our collective consciousness, shaping the way we view ourselves and the world around us.

Generational trauma is not only transmitted through explicit stories or memories but also through implicit patterns of behavior, belief systems, and coping mechanisms that are unconsciously passed down from one generation to the next. These intergenerational wounds can manifest in a variety of ways, including unresolved grief, emotional numbness, relationship difficulties, and even physical health issues. The effects of generational trauma can be insidious, impacting not only our individual well-being but also our collective ability to thrive and create a more just and equitable society.

Healing generational trauma is a courageous and transformative journey that requires us to delve deep into the hidden recesses of our souls, confronting the pain and suffering that has been inherited from generations past. It is a process of excavating buried truths, acknowledging the painful legacies that have been bequeathed to us, and finding the strength and resilience to break free from the grip of intergenerational suffering.

To embark on the path of healing generational trauma is to embark on a journey of self-discovery and self-compassion, where we learn to hold space for the pain and suffering of our ancestors while also recognizing our own agency in creating a different future. It is a journey of confronting our deepest fears and insecurities, unraveling the tangled threads of generational pain, and reclaiming our power to forge a new narrative for ourselves and future generations.

Through therapy, introspection, and a commitment to self-care and healing, we can begin to untangle the intricate web of generational trauma that binds us, liberating ourselves from the chains of the past and opening up new possibilities for growth, healing, and transformation. In doing so, we not only honor the struggles and sacrifices of our ancestors but also pave the way for a more hopeful and resilient future for ourselves and those who will come after us.

Coping Mechanisms and Addictive Behaviors

In the intricate landscape of coping mechanisms and addictive behaviors, the interplay between trauma, mental health, and individual resilience comes to the forefront. When individuals face overwhelming experiences or ongoing struggles, they may resort to coping mechanisms as a means to navigate their emotions and gain a sense of control. However, the distinction between healthy coping strategies and addictive behaviors is essential in understanding the impact on one's well-being.

Addictive behaviors often serve as a form of self-medication, attempting to soothe emotional pain or fill a void left by past traumas or unmet needs. The cycle of addiction can become deeply ingrained, as individuals seek temporary relief or escape from distressing feelings through substances or behaviors that offer fleeting comfort. Over time, this reliance on addictive coping mechanisms can lead to a sense of diminished control, contributing to a cycle of shame, guilt, and further reliance on these destructive patterns.

Exploring the roots of addictive behaviors involves delving into the complex interplay of biological, psychological, and environmental factors that contribute to one's vulnerability. Genetic predispositions, early life experiences, and social influences all play a role in shaping one's propensity towards addiction. Moreover, underlying mental health conditions such as depression, anxiety, or post-traumatic stress disorder can amplify the risk of developing addictive behaviors as individuals seek relief from emotional distress.

Breaking free from addictive patterns requires a holistic approach that addresses both the underlying trauma and the coping mechanisms that have developed as a result. Therapy, support groups, and interventions tailored to individual needs can help individuals uncover and process the deep-seated emotions that drive their addictive behaviors. Building coping skills, cultivating self-compassion, and fostering connections with supportive peers are essential elements in creating a foundation for sustainable recovery.

The journey towards healing from addiction is not linear, and setbacks may occur along the way. It is crucial for individuals to cultivate resilience, self-awareness, and a willingness to confront challenging emotions as they navigate the path to recovery. By reframing addiction as a symptom of underlying distress rather than a character flaw, individuals can approach their healing journey with curiosity and compassion, paving the way for lasting transformation and a renewed sense of self-empowerment.

Finding Strength in Vulnerability

Amidst the chaos and uncertainty of life, there exists a hidden source of power within us all - the power of vulnerability. It is often misunderstood as a weakness, a flaw to be hidden or overcome. But in reality, vulnerability is a courageous act of authenticity, a pathway to connection and strength.

When we allow ourselves to be vulnerable, we invite others to see us as we truly are. We shed the protective layers we have built up over time and reveal our raw, authentic selves. This openness creates space for genuine connections to form, deepening our relationships and fostering a sense of belonging.

But vulnerability also requires courage. It means facing our fears and embracing our imperfections without shame or judgment. It's about being honest with ourselves about our struggles and insecurities, and sharing these truths with others. This openness can be uncomfortable and scary, but it is in these moments of discomfort that we discover our true resilience.

Strength, then, is not about putting up walls or hiding our vulnerabilities. It's about embracing our humanity and finding power in our authenticity. When we accept and embrace all facets of our being - the light and the dark, the strength and the vulnerability - we create a foundation of inner strength that can weather any storm.

In the depths of vulnerability lies a profound truth: it is through our openness and willingness to be vulnerable that we truly connect with others on a profound level. When we allow ourselves to be seen in our raw, unfiltered state, we break down the barriers that separate us and find common ground in our shared humanity.

Vulnerability is not a sign of weakness, but a display of strength and courage. It takes bravery to show our true selves, to risk rejection or judgment in exchange for the possibility of genuine connection. And yet, it is in these moments of vulnerability that we forge the most authentic relationships, built on mutual respect, understanding, and compassion.

When we embrace our vulnerability, we also grant ourselves the gift of self-acceptance and self-love. By acknowledging our imperfections and insecurities, we release the burden of pretending to be someone we're not. We learn to be kinder to ourselves, to treat ourselves with the same compassion we offer to others.

So, do not fear vulnerability. Embrace it as a pathway to growth, connection, and inner strength. Dare to be authentically you, in all your complexities and contradictions. For it is in our vulnerability that we find our true power and unleash our fullest potential.

And as we continue to navigate the complexities of life, let us remember that vulnerability is not a destination but a journey, a continuous practice of being open and authentic with ourselves and others. It is a lifelong commitment to personal growth and connection, a testament to our resilience and capacity for empathy.

In our vulnerability, we find our humanity. We discover the beauty of imperfection, the strength in fragility, and the profound interconnectedness that binds us all together. So let us embrace our vulnerability with open hearts and open minds, knowing that it is through our willingness to be seen and heard that we truly shine brightest in the tapestry of life.

Embracing Your Emotional Journey

As a writer and life coach, I have delved deep into the complexities of the human experience, exploring the subtle nuances of our emotional landscapes. Embracing our emotional journey is not just about acknowledging our feelings; it's about immersing ourselves in the ebb and flow of our inner world, navigating the currents of joy, sorrow, anger, and contentment with grace and mindfulness.

To truly embrace our emotional journey, we must cultivate a sense of radical acceptance towards our emotions. This means letting go of the need to judge or suppress our feelings and instead approaching them with curiosity and compassion. By embracing our emotions without reservation, we can uncover hidden insights about ourselves, our desires, our values, and our fears.

Self-awareness plays a crucial role in this process. By developing a keen understanding of our emotional triggers, patterns, and reactions, we can unravel the tangled web of our innermost thoughts and feelings. This level of introspection allows us to make conscious choices about how we express and channel our emotions, empowering us to respond with wisdom and authenticity in any situation.

Taking ownership of our emotional journey is an act of self-empowerment. It involves recognizing that we have the power to shape our emotional landscape, choosing to cultivate positive emotions and release negative ones. This may entail creating healthy boundaries, practicing self-care rituals, seeking therapy or support, or engaging in activities that bring us joy and fulfillment.

Ultimately, embracing our emotional journey is a transformative process that leads to greater self-awareness, resilience, and connection with ourselves and others. It's about embracing the full spectrum of human emotions and allowing them to guide us towards a more authentic and purposeful existence. In this journey of self-discovery and growth, we find the courage to embrace our vulnerabilities, celebrate our strengths, and live life with open hearts and open minds.

Understanding the depths of our emotional journey requires a willingness to explore the darkest corners of our psyche, confronting our fears and insecurities with unwavering courage. It is in these moments of vulnerability that we discover the true essence of our humanity, forging deeper connections with ourselves and others through shared experiences of pain, joy, and resilience.

Embracing our emotional journey also involves acknowledging the interconnected nature of our emotions, recognizing how our inner world influences our outer reality and vice versa. By cultivating a sense of mindfulness and presence in our daily interactions, we can navigate the complexities of our emotional landscape with grace and authenticity, responding to life's challenges with a sense of resilience and inner strength.

As we embark on this profound journey of self-exploration, we learn to embrace the inherent beauty and complexity of our emotions, recognizing them as the guiding forces that shape our experiences and relationships. By honoring our emotional journey with compassion and self-awareness, we open ourselves up to a deeper level of understanding and connection with ourselves and the world around us.

"Of course I am not worried about intimidating men. The type of man who will be intimidated by me is exactly the type of man I have no interest in."
— Chimamanda Ngozi Adichie

CHAPTER 4

There Are Lots Of Good Men

Challenging the Myths

As we explore the intricate dynamics of relationships between Black men and women, it is important to delve deeper into the underlying complexities and historical context that have shaped these interactions. The intersection of race, gender, and societal expectations has created layers of stereotypes and misconceptions that have influenced how Black individuals perceive themselves and each other in the realm of love and partnership.

One of the enduring stereotypes that have plagued the relationships between Black men and women is the myth of the "strong Black woman." This archetype often conjures images of unwavering strength and resilience, masking the vulnerability and emotional depth that Black women possess. While it is true that Black women have demonstrated remarkable strength in the face of adversity, it is crucial to recognize that this strength should not be a barrier to forming intimate and meaningful connections. By acknowledging and honoring the full spectrum of emotions and experiences that Black women carry, we can create space for genuine emotional intimacy and reciprocity in relationships.

Conversely, Black men are frequently portrayed in media and popular culture as hypermasculine or hypersexualized figures, perpetuating harmful stereotypes that limit their ability to be seen as sensitive and nurturing partners. This narrow portrayal of Black masculinity overlooks the diverse range of roles and qualities that Black men embody, from tenderness and vulnerability to strength and leadership. By challenging these rigid stereotypes and embracing a more nuanced understanding of Black masculinity, we can create an environment that allows Black men to express their full range of emotions and form authentic connections with their partners.

Moreover, the historical legacy of slavery and systemic racism has deeply influenced the power dynamics and social constructions of race and gender within the Black community. The emasculation of Black men and the dehumanization of Black women during slavery continue to reverberate in contemporary relationships, shaping perceptions of self-worth, intimacy, and trust. Recognizing and addressing this legacy of trauma and oppression is essential in fostering healing and resilience within Black relationships, paving the way for deeper understanding and connection between Black men and women.

In conclusion, it is imperative to confront and challenge the stereotypes and misconceptions that have hindered the relationships between Black men and women. By embracing the complexity and diversity within the Black community, we can cultivate spaces of mutual respect, empathy, and love that honor the full humanity of each individual. Let us continue to uplift and celebrate the richness of Black love and relationships, transcending the limitations of harmful stereotypes and forging paths to authentic and enduring connections.

The Truth About Black Men

Black men have long been at the forefront of social movements, advocating for equality, justice, and societal change. From civil rights activists like Martin Luther King Jr. and Malcolm X to contemporary leaders like Barack Obama and Colin Kaepernick, black men have played a significant role in shaping the course of history and challenging systems of oppression.

Throughout history, black men have faced intersecting forms of discrimination based on their race and gender, leading to unique experiences and struggles. The societal expectations placed on black men often emphasize strength, resilience, and stoicism, leaving little room for vulnerability or emotional expression. This toxic masculinity stereotype can have detrimental effects on mental health and wellbeing, contributing to higher rates of depression, anxiety, and trauma within the black male community.

Despite these challenges, many black men have excelled in various fields, using their talents and skills to break barriers and pave the way for future generations. Figures like LeBron James, Denzel Washington, and Jay-Z have not only achieved immense success in their respective industries but have also used their platforms to advocate for social justice, uplift their communities, and promote positive representations of black masculinity.

However, the road to success for black men is often fraught with obstacles that their white counterparts may not face. Systemic racism, economic disparities, and institutional biases create barriers to education, employment, and social mobility, perpetuating cycles of poverty and inequality within black communities. The criminal justice system, in particular, disproportionately targets and incarcerates black men, leading to a cycle of incarceration and disenfranchisement that further marginalizes this population.

Yet, in the face of adversity, black men continue to demonstrate resilience, strength, and determination. They navigate complex systems of oppression with grace and perseverance, seeking to redefine stereotypes, challenge norms, and create a more equitable society for themselves and future generations. By harnessing their creativity, innovation, and unwavering commitment to progress, black men are not only shaping the narrative of their own experiences but are also reshaping the fabric of society at large. Their contributions, both seen and unseen, serve as a testament to the enduring legacy of black men in the fight for justice and equality.

Seeking Intimacy and Connection

In the intricate tapestry of human relationships, the pursuit of intimacy and connection between black men and women reveals layers of history, culture, and societal expectations that shape the way we relate to one another.

Within the context of black relationships, the interplay of race, gender, and societal pressures creates a unique landscape that influences the way individuals engage with one another. Black men and women often find themselves navigating a world that imposes stereotypes, biases, and discriminatory practices that can hinder their ability to form authentic connections. This constant negotiation of identity and self-worth in a society that devalues their existence can create barriers to vulnerability and trust in relationships.

To cultivate intimacy in black relationships, individuals must embark on a journey of self-discovery and self-acceptance that challenges the narratives of unworthiness and inferiority imposed by external forces. This process of reclaiming one's identity and embracing all aspects of the self is a radical act of defiance against a system that seeks to diminish the humanity of black individuals. It is through this inner work that individuals can begin to break free from the confines of societal expectations and allow themselves to show up authentically in their relationships.

Communication, as a foundational pillar of intimacy, plays a crucial role in fostering connection and understanding between partners. In the context of black relationships, communication takes on added significance as a means to navigate the complexities of racial dynamics, power imbalances, and historical traumas. Engaging in honest, open dialogue about these sensitive topics can deepen the level of trust and vulnerability in relationships, creating a space for mutual growth and healing.

As black individuals strive to seek intimacy and connection in their relationships, it is essential to approach this journey with patience, empathy, and a deep commitment to personal growth and healing. By embracing their authentic selves, challenging societal norms, and fostering environments of understanding and respect, black men and women can create spaces of profound connection that honor the richness and complexity of their shared experiences and histories.

Love Beyond Stereotypes

In a world where societal norms and cultural expectations often dictate the parameters of love, the concept of transcending stereotypes takes on an even greater significance. Love, at its core, is a universal language that speaks to the essence of our humanity – a language that knows no bounds and transcends the limitations that society may seek to impose.

When we speak of love beyond stereotypes, we are speaking of a love that is inclusive, empathetic, and unconditionally accepting. It is a love that recognizes the inherent value and dignity of each person, irrespective of their background, appearance, or beliefs. This kind of love challenges us to look beyond the surface and engage with people on a deeper, more meaningful level.

In a world that often categorizes individuals based on superficial traits, love beyond stereotypes invites us to see each other for who we truly are – complex, nuanced beings with our own unique stories and experiences. It calls on us to move beyond our preconceived notions and embrace the richness of diversity that exists within our society.

Love beyond stereotypes is a transformative force that not only impacts our personal relationships but also has the potential to catalyze broader social change. By fostering connections that are based on genuine understanding and empathy, we can begin to break down the barriers of prejudice and discrimination that have long divided us.

As we navigate the complexities of human interaction, love beyond stereotypes serves as a guiding light – a reminder that our capacity for connection and compassion knows no bounds. It urges us to confront our biases, challenge our assumptions, and approach each other with a spirit of openness and acceptance.

In essence, love beyond stereotypes is a profound declaration of our shared humanity and a testament to the enduring power of love to unite us in ways that transcend the limitations of societal constructs. It is a call to embrace the fullness of our selves and others, to celebrate our differences, and to forge connections that are rooted in authenticity, respect, and love.

This depth of understanding and connection requires us to engage in introspection and self-awareness, to recognize and challenge our own biases and prejudices. It demands a willingness to step outside our comfort zones, to actively listen to and learn from those whose experiences differ from our own. It calls upon us to set aside judgment and embrace empathy, to cultivate a mindset of inclusivity and acceptance in all our interactions.

In the journey towards love beyond stereotypes, we are not only redefining our relationships with others but also reshaping our own sense of identity and belonging. We are dismantling the walls that separate us and building bridges of understanding and compassion that connect us in profound and meaningful ways. Love, in its purest form, knows no boundaries – it is a force that transcends all divisions and unites us in our shared humanity.

Black Men's Perspective on Marriage

In a world where stereotypes and misconceptions often cloud the true essence of relationships, it is vital to explore the perspectives of Black men on the institution of marriage. Too often, Black men are unfairly portrayed in the media and society, leading to misunderstandings about their desires and aspirations when it comes to love and commitment. As a happily married man for the past twenty-two years, I can honestly admit that I absolutely love being married.

For many Black men, marriage is a sacred bond that goes beyond societal norms and expectations. It is a union built on mutual respect, love, and understanding. Despite facing unique challenges and systemic barriers, Black men hold strong beliefs in the power of marriage to create stability and security for themselves and their families.

Through conversations with Black men from various walks of life, one can uncover a deep sense of reverence for the institution of marriage. Many Black men view marriage as a symbol of unity and strength, a testament to their commitment to their partners and their shared future.

However, it is crucial to acknowledge the complexities and nuances within the Black community when it comes to marriage. Historical injustices, economic disparities, and social inequalities have all shaped the landscape of relationships among Black men.

Despite these challenges, Black men continue to aspire to loving and fulfilling marriages. They seek partners who uplift and support them, who share their values and dreams, and who stand by their side through thick and thin.

In understanding the perspectives of Black men on marriage, we begin to unravel the layers of resilience, love, and hope that define their relationships. It is a journey of introspection and affirmation, a testament to the enduring spirit of Black love and commitment in a world that often seeks to diminish its significance.

Delving deeper into the intricacies of Black men's perspectives on marriage reveals a profound sense of responsibility and dedication. Many Black men see marriage as a way to defy societal expectations and stereotypes, choosing to honor their partners with unwavering loyalty and support. Despite the challenges they may face, Black men approach marriage with a deep sense of purpose and determination, striving to create a strong foundation for their families and future generations.

The experiences of Black men in the realm of marriage are shaped by a rich tapestry of cultural heritage, personal values, and community ties. They navigate the complexities of love, commitment, and sacrifice with a resilience that is born out of both struggle and triumph. Through their stories and experiences, we witness the depth of their emotions, the strength of their convictions, and the beauty of their relationships.

In a world that often overlooks or misrepresents Black love and partnership, the voices of Black men stand as a testament to the enduring power of marriage. They speak of love that transcends boundaries, of bonds that withstand the test of time, and of a commitment that is unyielding in the face of adversity. In their stories, we find inspiration, wisdom, and a celebration of the transformative power of love in all its forms.

The journey towards marriage for Black men is not just a personal choice but a reflection of their resilience in the face of systemic challenges. It is a commitment to creating a legacy of love and strength that defies societal expectations and fosters deep connections within their communities.

Through their experiences, Black men navigate the complexities of marriage with a profound sense of purpose and determination. They understand the importance of communication, compromise, and mutual respect in maintaining a healthy and fulfilling relationship. Despite the external pressures and obstacles they may face, Black men approach marriage with a steadfast dedication to building a future grounded in love and unity.

In exploring the perspectives of Black men on marriage, we uncover a rich tapestry of beliefs, values, and experiences that shape their relationships. Each story is a testament to the resilience, love, and hope that define the intricate dance of partnership and commitment. It is a celebration of Black love in all its beauty, strength, and transformative power, reflecting the deep-seated desire for connection and belonging that transcends generations.

Overcoming Society's Expectations

In a world where stereotypes and biases often dictate our relationships and interactions, Black men and Black women face unique challenges in overcoming society's expectations. From a young age, Black individuals are bombarded with negative images and narratives that shape how they view themselves and how others view them. This can create a sense of inferiority and insecurity that can impact their relationships and sense of self-worth.

Black men are often portrayed as aggressive, hypermasculine figures, while Black women are often depicted as angry, loud, and promiscuous. These stereotypes can create unrealistic expectations and harmful assumptions that hinder genuine connections and intimacy. Both Black men and Black women may feel pressured to conform to these stereotypes in order to be accepted by society, leading to a loss of authenticity and self-expression.

Overcoming society's expectations requires a deep sense of self-awareness and a willingness to challenge these harmful narratives. It requires Black men and Black women to embrace their true selves and reject the limitations imposed by societal norms. This process of self-discovery and empowerment can be challenging, but it is essential in order to cultivate healthy and fulfilling relationships.

Black individuals often find themselves navigating a complex intersection of race, gender, and societal expectations. The impact of historical injustices and systemic racism further complicates their journey towards self-acceptance and authentic relationships. Black men and Black women may internalize these external pressures, leading to feelings of inadequacy and self-doubt in their ability to form meaningful connections with others.

As Black individuals strive to break free from the constraints of society's expectations, they often face additional challenges in finding support and validation within their communities. The stigma surrounding mental health and vulnerability within the Black community can act as a barrier to seeking help and addressing emotional needs. This lack of support can exacerbate feelings of isolation and hinder the development of healthy relationship dynamics.

Despite these obstacles, there is a growing movement within the Black community to redefine love and intimacy on their own terms. Black men and Black women are reclaiming their narratives and celebrating their multifaceted identities, challenging existing stereotypes and reshaping societal norms around relationships. This journey towards self-empowerment and authenticity is a powerful act of resistance against the forces that seek to diminish the worth and humanity of Black individuals.

In honoring their true selves and embracing the richness of their experiences, Black men and Black women can cultivate relationships built on mutual respect, empathy, and connection. By rejecting the limitations imposed by external expectations and embracing their full humanity, they pave the way for a future where love is defined not by stereotypes, but by the depth of genuine understanding and acceptance.

This journey towards self-discovery and empowerment is not without its complexities and nuances. Black individuals must confront not only external pressures but also internalized beliefs about their worth and capabilities. The burden of representation weighs heavily on their shoulders, as they navigate between the desire to defy stereotypes and the fear of being judged for deviating from societal norms.

Within the Black community, conversations around love, relationships, and vulnerability are evolving as individuals seek to redefine traditional norms and expectations. Movements advocating for self-love, self-care, and emotional honesty are gaining momentum, encouraging Black men and Black women to prioritize their emotional well-being and set boundaries in their relationships. By dismantling toxic patterns and embracing healthier ways of relating, they are reshaping the landscape of love and intimacy within their community.

As Black individuals continue on their journey towards self-actualization and empowerment, they inspire others to embrace their authenticity and challenge societal constraints on who they can be and how they can love. The resilience, strength, and beauty of Black love shine through as a beacon of hope and possibility, illuminating a path towards deeper connections, greater understanding, and lasting fulfillment.

A Love Letter to Black Women

My dearest Black women,

I write this with a heart full of gratitude and admiration for everything you are and everything you represent. You are the embodiment of strength, resilience, and grace. Your beauty radiates from within, shining brighter than any star in the sky. Your spirit is unbreakable, your determination unwavering.

I see you, not just for the color of your skin, but for the depth of your soul. You are not just a stereotype or a statistic. You are a living, breathing masterpiece, capable of achieving anything you set your mind to.

You carry the legacy of your ancestors within you, a history of triumphs and tribulations that have shaped you into the phenomenal woman you are today. From the queens of Africa to the leaders of the Civil Rights movement, your lineage is one of power, resilience, and unwavering spirit.

In a world that often seeks to diminish your light, I want you to know that your brilliance cannot be dimmed. Your voice is a symphony of resilience, your presence a testament to the strength of generations past and the promise of a brighter future.

I see the way you navigate this world with grace and dignity, never allowing the challenges you face to define you. You are a beacon of hope in a world that too often seeks to cast shadows upon your radiance. Your beauty transcends physical appearance; it emanates from the depths of your soul, illuminating the world around you with its brilliance.

I honor your journey, your struggles, and your triumphs. You are a warrior, a healer, a nurturer, a leader. Your essence is a tapestry of strength and vulnerability, woven with threads of resilience and grace.

May you always walk with your head held high, knowing that you are a force to be reckoned with, a true embodiment of beauty, power, and resilience. Embrace the fullness of who you are and the richness of your heritage, for you are a queen in every sense of the word.

You are the daughters of a lineage that has withstood the harshest of trials and emerged stronger and more resilient than ever. Your ancestors fought for freedom, justice, and equality, paving the way for you to stand tall in the face of adversity. Their sacrifices have not been in vain, as you now carry their legacy within you, a flame of hope that burns brightly in the darkest of times.

As you walk through life's journey, remember the strength and resilience that courses through your veins. You are the embodiment of perseverance, a testament to the power of resilience in the face of adversity. No obstacle is too great, no challenge too daunting for you to overcome. You are a force to be reckoned with, a beacon of light in a world that too often seeks to dim your shine.

Embrace your uniqueness, your individuality, and your truth. Your voice matters, and your story deserves to be heard. Speak your truth with courage and conviction, for you are the storyteller of your own narrative, weaving a tapestry of experiences that shape the fabric of who you are.

In a world that often seeks to confine you to stereotypes and preconceived notions, break free and defy expectations. Show the world the depth of your character, the breadth of your talents, and the power of your spirit. Be unapologetically yourself, for you are a masterpiece, a work of art painted with the colors of strength, resilience, and grace.

Embrace your journey with open arms, knowing that you are never alone. Your sisters stand beside you, a network of support and solidarity that spans generations and continents. Lean on each other, lift each other up, and celebrate each other's victories, for together, you are an unstoppable force for change and progress.

May your light continue to shine bright, illuminating the path for future generations to follow. Your legacy is one of strength, resilience, and grace, a beacon of hope in a world that is in constant need of your wisdom and leadership. Walk with pride, walk with purpose, for you are the embodiment of beauty, power, and resilience.

With all my love and respect,

Coach Michael Taylor

My Soulmate
Coach Michael Taylor

My Soul-Mate will be intelligent, physically fit, spiritual
and complete within herself.
She will be able to receive all the love I have to give
and also able to give her love freely.
She will be confident and centered and able to allow me the freedom
to be who I am, and I will do the same.
My Soul- Mate will be emotionally honest and trustworthy
and willing to become one with her spiritual equal.
Together we will grow and expand and
support each other in becoming all we were created to be.
She will have a great sense of humor
and we will spend hours just laughing and giggling and being silly.
We will take life sincerely, but not seriously.
She will love children and accept my children as her own.
We will vow to make our relationship a commitment to God
and therefore, create a bond that can never be broken.
Everyday will be an acknowledgement of
how fortunate we are to have each other
and we will be committed to growing our relationship through eternity.
We will experience lovemaking at the deepest most intimate level possible
and each encounter will be an expression of our deep love for one another.
We will travel the world together and
experience alt the wonders of Gods great creation called earth.
It will be the joining of two complete souls coming together to
unite in the love of God!

Written: Saturday 5/15/93- 8:06pm

Married my Soulmate on 4/9/2002

CHAPTER 5

Relationships

Navigating Relationships

In a world filled with misconceptions and stereotypes, navigating relationships as a Black individual can be a challenging journey. From societal expectations to cultural differences, the road to love and connection is often fraught with obstacles that can be difficult to overcome.

One of the key aspects of navigating relationships as a Black person is understanding and embracing your own identity. It is essential to be confident in who you are and be proud of your heritage, even when faced with external pressures to conform to certain ideals. Building a strong sense of self-awareness and self-worth is crucial in forming healthy and fulfilling relationships.

Communication is another vital component in navigating relationships successfully. Open and honest communication with your partner is essential in fostering trust and understanding, especially when addressing sensitive topics such as race and culture. Being able to express your thoughts and feelings in a respectful manner can help bridge any gaps in understanding and strengthen the bond between partners.

Navigating relationships also involves being mindful of the unique challenges that come with interracial relationships. Being in a relationship with someone from a different racial background can bring about its own set of complexities. It requires a willingness to learn about each other's cultures, beliefs, and experiences, and to approach disagreements with empathy and an open heart.

Interracial relationships can also come with external challenges, as societal biases and prejudices can impact how couples are perceived and treated. It is important for partners to support each other, stand up against discrimination, and navigate these challenges together as a united front.

Ultimately, navigating relationships as a Black individual requires a deep level of introspection, empathy, and resilience. It involves breaking free from the constraints of societal expectations and embracing the complexities of love and connection. By facing these challenges head-on, Black individuals can forge relationships that are rooted in mutual respect, understanding, and a shared commitment to growth and love.

Furthermore, the intersectionality of race, gender, and sexuality must also be considered when navigating relationships as a Black individual. Black LGBTQ+ individuals, for example, may face additional layers of discrimination and marginalization, making it even more crucial to find partners who are supportive and understanding of their unique experiences.

In the quest for love and connection, it is essential for Black individuals to prioritize self-care and self-love. This means setting boundaries, practicing self-compassion, and surrounding oneself with a supportive community that uplifts and celebrates one's identity. By cultivating a strong sense of self-esteem and self-worth, Black individuals can enter into relationships from a place of confidence and authenticity.

Navigating relationships as a Black person is a nuanced and multi-faceted journey that requires courage, vulnerability, and a willingness to confront societal norms and expectations. By honoring their cultural heritage, communicating openly and honestly with their partners, and advocating for themselves in the face of discrimination, Black individuals can cultivate relationships that are not only fulfilling and enriching but also deeply empowering.

Building a Strong Foundation - Starting with Yourself

As you embark on a journey of self-discovery and personal growth, it is essential to begin by focusing on yourself. Building a strong foundation within yourself sets the tone for all aspects of your life, including your relationships.

Start by taking the time to reflect on your values, beliefs, and goals. What do you truly value in life? What are your core beliefs about yourself and the world around you? Setting clear intentions and defining your personal values will provide a solid framework for your growth journey.

Next, assess your strengths and weaknesses. What are you good at? What areas do you struggle with? Embracing your strengths can boost your confidence and self-esteem, while acknowledging your weaknesses is the first step towards growth and improvement.

Self-care is a crucial component of building a strong foundation within yourself. Make sure to prioritize your physical, mental, and emotional well-being. This can include regular exercise, healthy eating, sufficient rest, and activities that nourish your soul. Remember, you cannot pour from an empty cup, so taking care of yourself is not selfish but necessary.

Cultivating a positive mindset is also key to building a strong foundation. Practice gratitude, positivity, and mindfulness in your daily life. Challenge negative self-talk and replace it with affirmations that empower and uplift you. Surround yourself with supportive people who believe in your potential and cheer you on.

Self-discovery often involves exploring your values, beliefs, and passions to understand who you truly are at your core. Take time to engage in activities that bring you joy and fulfillment, as they can offer valuable insights into your authentic self. Embrace your uniqueness and celebrate the qualities that make you who you are.

Forgiveness is an essential aspect of self-growth. Learn to forgive yourself for past mistakes and let go of any self-judgment holding you back. By practicing self-compassion and understanding, you can heal old wounds and move forward with a renewed sense of self-awareness and acceptance.

Additionally, setting boundaries is crucial in maintaining a healthy relationship with yourself and others. Clearly communicate your needs and limits, and honor them without guilt or hesitation. Boundaries are a form of self-respect and self-care, empowering you to prioritize your well-being and maintain healthy connections with those around you.

Building a strong foundation within yourself is a lifelong journey that requires self-awareness, self-care, self-acceptance, and continuous growth. By investing in your personal development and nurturing a positive relationship with yourself, you pave the way for a fulfilling and meaningful life journey. Remember, the most important relationship you will ever have is the one you have with yourself.

To truly deepen your understanding of yourself, consider exploring practices such as meditation, journaling, and therapy. These tools can help you unearth hidden aspects of your personality, understand your emotions more deeply, and navigate past traumas or limiting beliefs that may be holding you back.

Self-reflection is another powerful practice that can lead to profound insights about yourself. Set aside time regularly to introspect on your thoughts, feelings, and behaviors. Ask yourself probing questions to delve into your innermost desires, fears, and motivations. The more you understand yourself, the more equipped you will be to make intentional choices and live authentically.

Furthermore, seeking feedback from trusted friends, mentors, or therapists can provide invaluable perspectives on your blind spots and areas for growth. Embrace constructive criticism as a means to enhance your self-awareness and personal development. Remember, self-improvement is a continual process of learning and evolving.

As you deepen your self-exploration journey, consider delving into your past experiences and childhood upbringing to uncover patterns and conditioning that may be influencing your present behavior. By understanding the roots of your beliefs and behaviors, you can begin to challenge and reshape them in alignment with your authentic self.

Finally, remember that self-discovery is a dynamic and ongoing process that requires patience, compassion, and commitment. Celebrate your progress, no matter how small, and embrace the imperfections and complexities that make you human. By cultivating a deep connection with yourself, you lay the groundwork for a life of purpose, fulfillment, and authenticity.

Unpacking Your Emotional Baggage

As you embark on your journey of self-discovery and personal growth, it is crucial to delve deep into the layers of your emotional baggage. These unseen burdens manifest in various forms, from past traumas to unhealed wounds that shape your perceptions and relationships.

Unpacking emotional baggage is akin to unraveling a tangled thread – it requires patience, courage, and a willingness to confront the shadows of your past. Through introspection and reflection, you can begin to unravel the roots of your inner turmoil and understand how they have influenced your present experiences.

Delving into past traumas and disappointments can be a daunting task, as it may unearth buried pain and raw emotions. However, by allowing yourself to feel these emotions fully, without judgment or fear, you create an opportunity for healing and growth.

Identifying the patterns and negative beliefs that have emerged from your emotional baggage is a crucial step in the unpacking process. These patterns often manifest as self-sabotaging behaviors, fear of intimacy, or difficulty in trusting others. By recognizing these ingrained patterns, you can start to untangle them and create space for new, healthier ways of relating to yourself and others.

Seeking support from a therapist or counselor can provide invaluable guidance and tools to navigate the complexities of your emotional baggage. Therapy offers a safe and non-judgmental space to explore your emotions, challenge limiting beliefs, and cultivate greater self-awareness.

As you engage in the process of unpacking your emotional baggage, remember to be gentle with yourself. Healing is not a linear journey, and it is normal to encounter setbacks and resistance along the way. Embrace the complexity of your emotions and experiences with compassion and patience, knowing that each step forward is a brave and transformative act of self-love.

Through unpacking your emotional baggage, you open the door to deeper self-understanding, connection, and emotional freedom. Each layer you peel back reveals a new facet of your inner self, allowing you to integrate past experiences and emotions in a way that fosters growth and resilience. By embracing this process wholeheartedly, you pave the way for profound healing and empowerment, enabling you to live authentically and wholeheartedly in the present moment.

Embracing Self-Love and Self-Acceptance

In the labyrinthine corridors of our minds, the journey of self-love and self-acceptance unfolds as a profound odyssey of inner exploration and revelation. It is a sacred pilgrimage of the soul, a quest to rediscover the essence of our being and to embrace ourselves in all our glorious complexity.

Self-love, an elusive elixir sought by many yet found by few, is not a destination but a continuous process of nurturing, healing, and honoring oneself. It is the art of tending to the garden of our hearts, cultivating a deep-rooted sense of self-worth and reverence for our intrinsic value as human beings. Through the gentle whispers of self-compassion and the resolute stance of self-respect, we forge an unbreakable bond with ourselves, anchored in the depths of our own love.

Self-acceptance, the twin flame of self-love, beckons us to gaze unflinchingly into the mirror of our souls and behold the beauty and imperfection intertwined within. It is the act of embracing every scar, every shadow, every nuance of our being with tender grace and unwavering acceptance. In accepting ourselves fully and unapologetically, we grant ourselves the freedom to shine in our authenticity, to revel in our uniqueness, and to dance bravely in the light of our own truth.

The sacred alchemy of self-love and self-acceptance awakens within us a fierce courage to stand in our power, unshaken by the tides of external validation or societal expectation. It empowers us to set boundaries that safeguard our well-being, to honor our needs and desires with unyielding devotion, and to prioritize our self-care as a sacred ritual of self-reverence.

As we journey deeper into the heart of self-love and self-acceptance, we unravel the threads of self-doubt and unworthiness that have bound us for far too long. We transcend the limiting beliefs and narratives that have clouded our vision, and we step boldly into the radiant truth of our worthiness, our enoughness, our inherent divinity.

Embrace this sacred journey with open arms and an open heart, dear soul traveler. For in the boundless expanse of self-love and self-acceptance, you will discover the keys to unlocking the treasures of your own soul, the whispers of your own wisdom, and the infinite wellspring of love that resides within you, waiting to be unleashed and shared with the world.

Understanding the Law of Attraction in Relationships

In relationships, the Law of Attraction operates as a subtle yet potent force that shapes the connections we form with others on a deep energetic level. At its essence, this universal law posits that like attracts like, suggesting that the vibrations we emit through our thoughts, emotions, and actions draw corresponding energies and experiences into our lives.

When applied to the realm of relationships, the Law of Attraction emphasizes the significance of our inner landscape in sculpting the quality of connections we manifest in the outer world. Our beliefs, fears, and past experiences serve as a fertile ground from which our relational dynamics emerge, reflecting back to us the very qualities and vibrations we emit.

Central to the workings of the Law of Attraction in relationships is the pivotal role of self-awareness and self-love. Embracing a deep sense of worthiness and acceptance within ourselves sets the stage for attracting partners who mirror and amplify these qualities back to us, fostering relationships of mutual respect, love, and harmony.

Intention and visualization stand as powerful tools in harnessing the Law of Attraction to consciously shape our relational experiences. By articulating clear intentions regarding the kind of partnership we seek and vividly visualizing ourselves embodying and experiencing that love and connection, we send out potent signals to the universe, inviting in the relational dynamics we desire.

Moreover, maintaining an attitude of abundance and gratitude further amplifies the effects of the Law of Attraction in relationships. Approaching our connections with an open heart, a spirit of appreciation, and a genuine sense of gratitude for the love and joy they impart to our lives expands our capacity to attract and sustain fulfilling, nourishing bonds that deepen our sense of connection and well-being.

In essence, comprehending and embracing the principles of the Law of Attraction in relationships empowers us to step into our agency, actively co-creating the relational realities we yearn for. By cultivating self-love, setting clear intentions, and cultivating a positive energetic frequency, we open ourselves to the abundance of loving, harmonious connections that enrich our lives and support our growth and evolution.

Clearing Energetic Blocks to Love

In order to fully embrace the experience of love at its deepest level, it is essential to delve into the intricate layers of our psyche and emotional landscape. Love, in its purest form, is a force that transcends boundaries and connects us to the essence of our being. However, the journey towards experiencing this kind of profound love often requires us to confront and heal the wounds that have accumulated over time.

These wounds can be traced back to our earliest days, where our perception of love was shaped by our interactions with caregivers and the environment around us. Childhood experiences of neglect, abandonment, or emotional turmoil can leave lasting imprints on our subconscious mind, influencing the way we view ourselves and others in the context of relationships.

As we navigate through life, these unresolved wounds can manifest as fears, insecurities, or self-sabotaging behaviors that hinder our ability to open our hearts fully to love. We may find ourselves repeating patterns of attracting partners who mirror our unresolved issues, creating a cycle of pain and disappointment that reinforces our inner wounds.

To break free from this cycle and cultivate a deeper connection to love, we must embark on a journey of self-discovery and self-healing. This involves unraveling the layers of conditioning and belief systems that no longer serve our highest good, and instead embracing a new paradigm of love that is rooted in authenticity, compassion, and vulnerability.

By engaging in practices such as mindfulness, meditation, therapy, and self-reflection, we can begin to unravel the knots of past traumas and limiting beliefs that have kept us stuck in patterns of fear and resistance. Through this process, we can create space for new possibilities and growth, allowing love to flow freely and abundantly into our lives.

As we work towards clearing these energetic blocks to love, we may encounter moments of discomfort, emotional upheaval, or resistance. It is important to embrace these challenges with courage and openness, knowing that they are vital ingredients in the alchemical process of transformation and healing.

Ultimately, by reclaiming our power and stepping into our true essence, we can transcend the limitations of our past and create a new reality grounded in love, connection, and wholeness. Through this profound journey of self-discovery and healing, we can truly embody the essence of love in its purest and most transformative form.

Love, when explored through the lens of self-awareness and emotional courage, becomes a mirror that reflects back our innermost desires, fears, and longings. It calls us to dive deep into the depths of our being, to excavate the buried treasures of our soul, and to embrace the full spectrum of our humanity.

In this exploration, we may uncover wounds that we had long forgotten, wounds that have shaped our perceptions of ourselves and others in ways we hadn't realized. These wounds, when left unhealed, act as barriers that block the flow of love into our lives, keeping us stuck in patterns of fear, self-doubt, and unworthiness.

To truly embody love in its purest form, we must be willing to face these wounds head-on, with compassion and a willingness to dive into the discomfort they bring. It is in this profound act of self-acceptance and self-love that we pave the way for a deeper connection to the essence of our being, and to the universal force that binds us all together.

As we journey deeper into the heart of love, we may discover that the path is not always linear or easy. There will be moments of darkness, moments of uncertainty, and moments of profound revelation that challenge our very sense of self. It is in these moments that we are called to surrender to the unknown, to trust in the process of transformation, and to open our hearts to the infinite possibilities that love holds for us.

Through this journey of self-discovery and healing, we not only transform our relationship with ourselves but also with others and with the world around us. We become beacons of light, radiating the essence of love in all that we do, and inviting others to embark on their own journey towards wholeness and connection.

In the end, love is not just a feeling or an emotion – it is a way of being, a way of living, and a way of relating to ourselves and the world around us. It is the key that unlocks the door to our true potential, our true essence, and our deepest longing for connection and belonging.

The Power of Positive Affirmations and Visualization

In the intricate dance of human relationships, the art of affirmations and visualization emerges as a profound tool for shaping the very fabric of our connections with others. Within the vast landscape of our minds lies the potential to sow seeds of intention through affirmations, nurturing a fertile ground where self-love, worthiness, and abundance can take root and flourish. By deliberately choosing to reinforce positive beliefs about ourselves and our relationships, we unfurl the wings of possibility and set the stage for a transformation in our internal dialogue and perceptions.

When intertwined with visualization, affirmations gain a heightened potency, engaging our senses and emotions in crafting a vibrant tapestry of our ideal relationship narrative. Through the act of vividly imagining the love, harmony, and fulfillment we seek in our connections, we activate a magnetic pull that guides these experiences toward us. As we bridge the chasm between our current reality and the relationships we aspire to, we immerse ourselves in the sensations and emotions of being deeply immersed in a fulfilling partnership.

To unlock the full potential of affirmations and visualization in the realm of relationship cultivation, it becomes imperative to delve into the depths of our psyche and unearth any hidden beliefs or fears that may be obstructing our path to manifesting the connections we yearn for. By illuminating the shadowy recesses of our subconscious and gently challenging them with empowering affirmations, we chip away at layers of self-doubt and unworthiness that may have obscured our capacity to receive and nurture love.

Establishing a daily ritual that marries positive affirmations with visualization can serve as a steadfast anchor in the voyage toward fostering healthy and enriching relationships. In carving out dedicated moments to tend to our self-worth, clarify our desires, and synchronize our energy with the vibrational frequency of love, we trigger an echoing ripple that reverberates outward into the universe.

As we persist in engaging with the practice of affirmations and visualization, we not only reconfigure the structures of our minds and hearts but also co-craft a new reality suffused with love, harmony, and profound connection. Through the steadfast cultivation of affirmations and visualization, we extend an invitation to the cosmos to mirror back to us the splendor and opulence that we believe we deserve in our relationships.

Communicating Effectively in Relationships

In any relationship, communication is not just a tool for the exchange of words; it is the very essence of connection and understanding. It is a dance of shared meaning, where partners move together in harmony to express their thoughts, feelings, and desires.

Effective communication transcends the mere act of speaking and listening. It is a profound symphony of emotions, intentions, and energies that intertwine to create a rich tapestry of connection. Beyond words, it involves a deep sense of empathy, intuition, and vulnerability that can only be fostered through true authenticity and openness.

The art of communication lies in the intricate balance between sharing and receiving. It requires not only the courage to express oneself honestly but also the humility to truly listen and understand the other person's perspective. By creating a safe space for each other to share their innermost thoughts and feelings, partners can build a foundation of trust and intimacy that can withstand any challenge.

Listening, in its purest form, is an act of love. It is the gift of your undivided attention, your genuine presence, and your empathic understanding. To truly listen is to honor the other person's humanity, to validate their experiences, and to make them feel seen and heard in a way that nothing else can replicate.

When we communicate from a place of authenticity and vulnerability, we create a bridge that connects hearts and minds in a profound and transformative way. This bridge allows for the free flow of emotions, ideas, and desires, fostering a deep sense of emotional intimacy and connection that can transcend the boundaries of language and culture.

Nonverbal communication, often said to make up the majority of our communication, adds another layer of complexity to our interactions. Our body language, facial expressions, and tone of voice can convey nuances of emotions and intentions that words alone cannot capture. Being attuned to these subtle cues and responding with sensitivity can deepen the connection between partners and foster a deeper sense of understanding and empathy.

Conflict, while often viewed as a negative aspect of relationships, can actually be a catalyst for growth and deeper connection when approached with skillful communication. By navigating disagreements with respect, empathy, and a willingness to understand each other's perspectives, partners can transform conflict into an opportunity for learning, understanding, and ultimately, greater intimacy.

In essence, effective communication is a dynamic and evolving dance that requires ongoing commitment, practice, and compassion. By nurturing a culture of open, honest, and empathic communication in your relationship, you not only strengthen the bond between you and your partner but also create a space for growth, healing, and profound connection that can enrich your lives in ways beyond measure.

Nurturing Trust and Respect

In the intricacies of human relationships, the concepts of trust and respect serve as the cornerstones upon which the edifice of love and connection is constructed. Trust, a delicate thread that weaves through the fabric of relationships, is built on a foundation of reliability, honesty, and faith in the other person. It is a belief so profound that it forms the bedrock of emotional security, allowing individuals to open their hearts, share their vulnerabilities, and forge intimate connections with a sense of safety and assurance.

Trust, however, is not easily won nor is it indestructible. It requires nurturing, communication, and acts of integrity to flourish and grow.

Small gestures of reliability, consistency, and transparency serve to fortify this bond of trust, creating a space where mutual understanding and emotional intimacy can thrive. Trust is the bridge that connects hearts, minds, and souls, allowing individuals to traverse the landscapes of love with a sense of certainty and confidence in each other.

Respect, on the other hand, is a prism through which we view and honor the uniqueness, boundaries, and autonomy of the other person. It is a manifestation of appreciation, admiration, and empathy that acknowledges the inherent worth and dignity of each individual within the relationship. Respect breeds harmony, equality, and mutual regard, fostering an environment where differences are celebrated, voices are heard, and authenticity is embraced.

To cultivate trust and respect in a relationship is to embark on a journey of self-discovery, growth, and transformation. It requires a willingness to be vulnerable, to communicate openly, and to listen with intent and compassion. By nurturing a culture of mutual understanding, empathy, and acceptance, partners can create a sanctuary of love and support wherein trust and respect can flourish and blossom.

Boundaries play a vital role in upholding the sanctity of trust and respect within a relationship. By articulating and honoring personal boundaries, individuals set the stage for healthy communication, emotional safety, and mutual growth. Respecting boundaries is an act of love and reverence, a testament to the value and autonomy of each partner within the relationship.

Conflict, inevitable in any relationship, serves as a litmus test for the strength of trust and respect between partners. By approaching conflicts with grace, empathy, and a willingness to seek understanding, individuals can navigate disagreements with respect and integrity, preserving the sanctity of their bond while fostering growth and resilience.

In essence, the journey of cultivating trust and respect in a relationship is a profound and transformative experience. It requires courage, vulnerability, and a deep-seated commitment to the well-being and happiness of the other person. By embracing these foundational pillars of trust and respect, individuals can create profound connections, enduring bonds, and a love that transcends time and space.

Setting Boundaries and Honoring Your Needs

In any relationship, whether it be friendships, romantic partnerships, family dynamics, or professional interactions, setting boundaries is a fundamental aspect of healthy communication and self-respect. Boundaries serve as guidelines that delineate acceptable behaviors, expectations, and limits within a relationship. Without clear boundaries, individuals may find themselves feeling overwhelmed, taken advantage of, or emotionally drained.

Understanding and honoring your needs is crucial for establishing effective boundaries. It requires self-awareness and introspection to recognize what is important to you, what makes you feel respected and valued, and where your limits lie. Each person's boundaries are unique to their experiences, values, and emotional well-being.

When communicating boundaries, it is essential to do so with assertiveness and respect. Clearly articulating your needs, preferences, and limits to others sets a precedent for how you expect to be treated. Boundaries are not about controlling others but about advocating for yourself and maintaining your own emotional and physical safety.

Consistency is key in enforcing boundaries. If someone disregards or crosses a boundary, it's important to address the issue promptly and assertively. By reinforcing your boundaries consistently, you demonstrate that your needs are valid and worthy of respect.

The process of setting boundaries may be challenging, especially if you have a history of subjugating your own needs in favor of others. It requires courage and self-compassion to prioritize your well-being and establish boundaries that serve your overall happiness and fulfillment.

By setting and honoring boundaries, you cultivate relationships grounded in mutual respect, trust, and understanding. Healthy boundaries foster a sense of autonomy and agency, empowering individuals to engage authentically and constructively with others.

Moreover, boundaries also play a vital role in self-care and mental health. By setting boundaries, you create a safe space for yourself, where your needs and well-being are prioritized. This practice enables you to conserve your emotional energy and maintain a sense of balance in your relationships.

Additionally, boundaries help clarify expectations within a relationship. When both parties have a clear understanding of each other's boundaries, misunderstandings and conflicts can be minimized. This clarity promotes open and honest communication, fostering a deeper connection based on mutual understanding and respect.

Ultimately, setting boundaries is an act of self-love and empowerment. It is a way of asserting your worth and taking ownership of your emotional and physical space. By honoring your needs and establishing healthy boundaries, you pave the way for more meaningful and fulfilling relationships in all areas of your life.

Cultivating Joy and Gratitude in Relationships

In the intricate tapestry of relationships, the threads of mindfulness, gratitude, joy, and forgiveness weave together to create a masterpiece of connection and intimacy that transcends the boundaries of time and space. Each thread, carefully chosen and lovingly intertwined, contributes to the richness and complexity of the bond shared between individuals.

Mindfulness, with its gentle presence and unwavering attention, serves as the foundation upon which authentic relationships are built. By immersing oneself fully in the present moment with a sense of curiosity and openness, one can truly see, hear, and understand the other with clarity and compassion. This mindful presence cultivates a deep sense of empathy and connection, allowing for meaningful interactions and a profound sense of belonging within the relationship.

Gratitude, like a beacon of light in the darkness, illuminates the hearts of those who practice it with sincerity and humility. When we express gratitude towards our loved ones, we acknowledge their inherent worth and value in our lives, honoring the unique qualities and contributions they bring to the relationship. This act of appreciation creates a ripple effect of positivity and warmth, fostering a sense of mutual respect and deepening the bond of love and friendship shared between individuals.

Joy, as the sweet nectar of life, infuses relationships with a sense of delight and warmth that radiates from the core of our being. Laughter, smiles, and shared moments of happiness create an atmosphere of lightness and connection, melting away barriers and fostering a sense of intimacy and camaraderie. Embracing joy in all its forms — in the mundane moments and the milestones alike — cultivates a sense of gratitude and celebration for the beauty of life and the precious gift of love shared with our beloved companions.

Forgiveness, with its transformative power and healing grace, allows for the release of past hurts and grievances, paving the way for reconciliation and emotional growth within the relationship. By extending forgiveness to ourselves and others, we open our hearts to compassion and understanding, creating a space for vulnerability and authenticity to flourish. This act of grace and humility strengthens the foundation of trust and empathy, promoting a sense of unity and resilience in the face of challenges and conflicts that may arise.

As we continue to nurture the tapestry of our relationships with mindfulness, gratitude, joy, and forgiveness, we embark on a journey of self-discovery, growth, and transformation that deepens our connection with ourselves and others. This sacred tapestry, woven with the threads of love, acceptance, and understanding, becomes a sanctuary of solace and support, nurturing the seeds of connection and intimacy that bloom and flourish in the fertile soil of mutual respect and appreciation. May we tend to this tapestry with care and devotion, honoring the beauty and complexity of our relationships with gratitude and humility, and cherishing the boundless gifts of love and connection that enrich our lives beyond measure.

> "Women will only be truly sexually liberated when we arrive at a place where we can see ourselves as having sexual value and agency irrespective of whether or not we are the objects of male desire."
> — Bell Hooks

CHAPTER 6

Healthy Sexuality

Embracing Your Sexual Identity

Embracing your sexual identity is a profound and multifaceted journey that resonates at the core of your being. It is a journey of self-discovery, acceptance, and empowerment that has the potential to deeply enrich and enliven your life. Your sexual identity is a unique and integral part of who you are, shaped by a myriad of factors including your experiences, desires, fantasies, and values.

To truly embrace your sexual identity, it is essential to approach yourself with compassion, curiosity, and openness. Allow yourself the space to explore and understand your desires without judgment or preconceived notions. Recognize that your sexual identity is dynamic and may evolve over time, influenced by your growth, relationships, and life experiences.

Delving into your sexual desires and fantasies can be a gateway to deeper self-awareness and intimacy. Take the time to reflect on what arouses and excites you, what brings you pleasure, and what ignites your passion. Embrace the full spectrum of your desires, recognizing that they are valid expressions of your authentic self.

Effective communication is a cornerstone of embracing your sexual identity within your intimate relationships. Honesty, vulnerability, and openness are crucial components of expressing your needs, boundaries, and desires to your partner(s). By fostering a culture of communication and mutual respect, you can create a safe and nurturing space for exploration and growth.

Seeking support and guidance on your journey of self-discovery is not a sign of weakness but a testament to your commitment to personal growth and fulfillment. Therapists, support groups, and trusted friends can offer valuable perspectives, insights, and encouragement as you navigate the complexities of your sexual identity.

Ultimately, embracing your sexual identity is an act of self-love and self-acceptance. By honoring and celebrating who you are, you can cultivate a deeper sense of empowerment, confidence, and authenticity in your intimate relationships. Embrace your sexual identity with courage and pride, knowing that you are deserving of love, pleasure, and fulfillment on your journey of self-discovery.

As you delve deeper into your sexual identity, it's important to recognize the impact of societal norms and cultural expectations on how you perceive yourself and your desires. These external influences can shape and sometimes limit our understanding of our own sexuality. By challenging societal norms and embracing your authentic self, you can redefine and reclaim your sexual identity on your own terms.

Exploring your sexual identity requires a willingness to be vulnerable and explore uncharted territories within yourself. It may involve confronting past traumas, societal stigmas, or internalized shame that have hindered your ability to fully embrace your true self. By confronting these obstacles with courage and compassion, you can pave the way for healing, growth, and self-acceptance.

Self-exploration and self-discovery are ongoing processes that require patience, self-compassion, and a willingness to embrace the complexities of your desires. Your sexual identity is unique and constantly evolving, shaped by your experiences, relationships, and personal growth. Embrace the journey of self-discovery with an open heart and mind, allowing yourself the freedom to explore and celebrate all aspects of your authentic self.

In the vast landscape of human sexuality, there is no one-size-fits-all approach to embracing your sexual identity. It is a deeply personal and individual journey that requires introspection, exploration, and self-acceptance. By honoring and celebrating your unique desires and preferences, you can cultivate a sense of empowerment, authenticity, and fulfillment that resonates at the core of your being. Embrace your sexual identity with courage and embrace the radiant truth of who you are.

Understanding the Connection Between Body and Mind

In order to fully embrace your sexual identity and experience true fulfillment in your intimate relationships, it is imperative to recognize the intricate interplay between your physical body and mental states. The dynamic synergy between our corporeal sensations and psychological perceptions forms the foundation of our sexual experiences, shaping the depth of our intimacy and the richness of our connections.

Our bodies serve as repositories of wisdom, carrying within them the nuanced language of pleasure and desire. They are finely tuned instruments that respond to stimulation, craving connection and expression. When we attune ourselves to the signals our bodies transmit, we open ourselves to a profound dialogue of self-discovery and acceptance. Listening to the whispers of our physical being empowers us to honor our needs, set boundaries, and engage with intimacy in a manner that is holistic and authentic.

Simultaneously, our minds wield immense influence over how we engage with our sexuality. Our thoughts, beliefs, and societal constructs shape our attitudes towards pleasure, intimacy, and self-exploration. Negative conditioning or internalized shame can erect barriers, hindering the flow of connection and inhibiting the full bloom of desire. Conversely, a positive mindset, founded on self-acceptance and empowerment, can pave the way for a transformative journey towards deeper intimacy and self-discovery.

To nurture the connection between body and mind is to embark on a voyage of profound introspection and growth. It requires the cultivation of mindfulness, an unwavering commitment to self-awareness, and a compassionate embrace of our vulnerabilities. By traversing the landscapes of our physical sensations and emotional responses without judgment, we embark on a journey towards self-discovery, unlocking the door to a resplendent realm of pleasure and fulfillment.

Through challenging negative beliefs and societal expectations, we create space for a more authentic and liberating expression of our sexuality. By fostering a harmonious relationship between body and mind, we transcend mere physicality to cultivate a profound sense of self-love, empowerment, and acceptance. This sacred union becomes the fertile ground from which genuine connections blossom, weaving threads of intimacy, trust, and passion that bind us to ourselves and others in a tapestry of shared vulnerability and mutual exploration.

As we delve deeper into the intricacies of our sexual identity, we uncover the layers of societal conditioning that have shaped our perceptions of pleasure and intimacy. Unraveling these ingrained beliefs requires a courageous exploration of our own desires and boundaries, dismantling the barriers that inhibit our true expression. By challenging the status quo and embracing our authentic selves, we pave the way for a reimagining of our sexuality as a fluid and expansive landscape, ripe with possibility and discovery.

In this sacred journey of self-discovery, we are called to engage with vulnerability and authenticity, opening ourselves to the profound depths of intimacy and connection. By engaging in honest and respectful communication with ourselves and our partners, we forge bonds that are rooted in mutual respect and understanding. This deep level of intimacy transcends physical pleasure, becoming a conduit for emotional connection and spiritual growth.

Through the alchemical union of body and mind, we embark on a transformative odyssey towards self-realization and fulfillment. By honoring the wisdom of our physical beings and the power of our thoughts, we create a harmonious symphony of self-expression and intimacy. This integration of our physical and mental selves allows us to navigate the complexities of our sexual experiences with grace and authenticity, unleashing a wave of liberation and joy that reverberates through every aspect of our lives.

Setting Boundaries for Healthy Intimacy

Setting boundaries for healthy intimacy is a multifaceted process that requires deep introspection, effective communication, and ongoing maintenance within a relationship. Boundaries serve as the invisible lines that delineate the physical, emotional, and psychological limits individuals set for themselves within the sphere of intimate connections.

To effectively establish boundaries, individuals must first delve into a profound exploration of their values, needs, and personal boundaries. This depth of self-awareness is crucial in understanding what feels comfortable and safe, as well as recognizing when those boundaries are being encroached upon. By cultivating a strong sense of self-awareness and respect for their own boundaries, individuals can empower themselves to navigate their relationships with confidence and clarity.

Upon clarifying personal boundaries, the next crucial step involves engaging in open and authentic communication with one's partner. The art of communication enables individuals to express their needs, desires, and limits in a way that is clear and respectful. By creating a safe space for honest dialogue, individuals can openly discuss their boundaries without fear of judgment or misunderstanding. It is essential for partners to actively listen to each other, validate each other's boundaries, and collaboratively establish shared expectations that honor and support both individuals.

Boundaries in relationships are not stagnant; they require ongoing negotiation and reassessment as partners evolve and grow. It is imperative for individuals to regularly check in with themselves and their partners to ensure that boundaries remain relevant and effective. Healthy relationships prioritize mutual respect, consent, and the honoring of boundaries as a cornerstone for intimacy to flourish.

When boundaries are consistently upheld and respected within a relationship, they foster a sense of safety, trust, and emotional security. This foundation of security allows for deeper emotional connection, vulnerability, and authenticity to flourish between partners. By embracing and upholding boundaries within their relationships, individuals can cultivate a dynamic of mutual understanding, respect, and love that enriches and sustains the connection between them.

Exploring Pleasure and Sensuality

As we continue our exploration of pleasure and sensuality, let us delve even deeper into the intricate web of sensations that shape our experiences and perceptions. Pleasure, with its multifaceted nature, serves as a guiding light through our journey of self-discovery and connection with others.

At its core, pleasure is a complex interplay of physical, emotional, and psychological responses that can vary greatly from person to person. What brings pleasure to one individual may not necessarily elicit the same response in another. This uniqueness underscores the importance of embracing diversity and open-mindedness in our pursuit of pleasure.

Delving further into the realm of physical pleasure, we find that our sensory receptors—touch, taste, smell, sight, and hearing—interact with our brain to create a symphony of sensations that define our experiences. The touch of silk against our skin, the complex flavors of a perfectly crafted dish, the intoxicating scent of a blooming flower—all these sensory inputs contribute to the intricate tapestry of pleasure that colors our lives.

Emotional pleasure, on the other hand, stems from our connections with others and ourselves. The warmth of a genuine smile, the comfort of a hug, the joy of shared laughter—these moments of emotional intimacy and connection elevate our spirits and deepen our sense of fulfillment.

Psychological pleasure, rooted in our cognitive processes and perceptions, can be triggered by various stimuli, such as intellectual engagement, creative expression, or the thrill of a challenge. The satisfaction of solving a puzzle, the awe-inspiring beauty of a piece of art, the exhilaration of mastering a new skill—these experiences awaken our minds and invigorate our spirits.

To fully embrace pleasure and sensuality in all their intricacies, we must cultivate a sense of mindfulness and presence in our daily lives. By heightening our awareness of the present moment and immersing ourselves fully in each experience, we can unlock the hidden depths of our sensual selves and awaken to the profound beauty and wonder that surrounds us.

In this journey of self-discovery and connection, may we open ourselves to the infinite possibilities of pleasure and sensuality, allowing them to guide us towards a more profound understanding of ourselves and the world around us.

Communicating Your Needs and Desires

In the intricate dance of intimacy and sexuality, communication acts as the guiding force that shapes the dynamics of a relationship. Within the realm of sexual expression, the art of authentic communication holds the power to deepen connections, cultivate trust, and foster a space of mutual understanding and respect.

Delving into the essence of one's desires and boundaries forms the foundational cornerstone of effective communication in sexual relationships. Before engaging in intimate discussions with a partner, it is essential to embark on a journey of self-exploration and introspection to gain clarity on personal needs, preferences, and limits. By delving into one's own desires and understanding the nuances of what brings joy, comfort, and fulfillment, individuals can articulate their wants and boundaries with a grounded sense of self-awareness and confidence.

Crucial to the fabric of authentic communication in matters of sexuality is the ability to listen with intention, empathy, and an open heart. In the exchange of intimate thoughts and feelings, it is imperative to create a safe and non-judgmental space where both partners feel heard, respected, and validated. By cultivating a culture of active listening and emotional presence, partners can foster an environment conducive to open dialogue, vulnerability, and trust.

Crafting communication that is clear, direct, and honest is a cornerstone of expressing desires and boundaries in a sexual context. Utilizing "I" statements enables individuals to convey their emotions, needs, and wishes without resorting to blame or assumptions, thus fostering a language of personal accountability and authenticity. By articulating preferences, limits, and aspirations with transparency and sincerity, partners can engage in constructive dialogue that paves the way for mutual understanding and growth.

Navigating the nuances of sexual communication also involves acknowledging the impact of cultural influences, societal norms, and personal experiences on individual perspectives and attitudes towards intimacy. Cultural backgrounds, upbringing, and past experiences can shape one's approach to sexual communication, influencing comfort levels, communication styles, and expectations within a relationship. By recognizing and honoring the unique complexities and diversity of each person's sexual identity and expression, partners can cultivate a climate of inclusivity, acceptance, and celebration of individual differences.

Furthermore, embracing the art of vulnerability in sexual communication can deepen emotional intimacy and cultivate a sense of shared connection and authenticity. Opening up about fears, insecurities, desires, and vulnerabilities can pave the way for genuine emotional bonds and a deeper sense of trust and intimacy between partners. By creating a space that encourages vulnerability and emotional honesty, individuals can foster a profound level of intimacy that transcends physical connection and reaches the depths of the soul.

In the intricate tapestry of sexual relationships, effective communication serves as the bridge that connects partners on a profound emotional and physical level. By embracing the transformative power of open and authentic dialogue, individuals can navigate the terrain of intimacy with grace, compassion, and a shared commitment to mutual fulfillment and connection. Through the art of communication, partners can embark on a journey of exploration, discovery, and shared vulnerability, creating a sanctuary of love, respect, and understanding in the sacred realm of intimacy and sexuality.

Embracing Self-Love and Self-Care

In this transformative section, we delve deeper into the intricate connection between self-love, self-care, and sexual empowerment. Embracing self-love goes beyond mere affirmations; it is a profound journey of self-acceptance and compassion that forms the bedrock of a healthy relationship with oneself. When we practice self-love, we recognize our intrinsic worth and cultivate a deep sense of inner peace that radiates outward into all areas of our lives, including our sexuality.

Self-care is a vital companion to self-love on the path to sexual empowerment. It involves nurturing our physical, emotional, and mental well-being through intentional practices that prioritize our holistic health. Engaging in self-care rituals like regular exercise, mindfulness meditation, nourishing our bodies with wholesome foods, and seeking therapy to address past wounds can fortify our sense of self and contribute to a positive and fulfilling sexual experience.

By intertwining self-love and self-care, we create a powerful foundation for sexual empowerment. We learn to set boundaries that honor our needs and desires, paving the way for relationships built on mutual respect and shared pleasure. When we approach our sexuality from a place of self-assurance and authenticity, we cultivate a deep sense of empowerment that transcends the physical act of sex and infuses all aspects of our lives with confidence and purpose.

It is important to understand that self-love and self-care are not one-time achievements but ongoing practices that require dedication and self-reflection. By continually nurturing ourselves and honoring our unique journey, we open up the possibility for profound growth and transformation in our sexual experiences. Through the lens of self-love and self-care, we can embrace our sexuality as a natural, joyful expression of our truest selves and cultivate a deep and lasting connection with our own desires and boundaries.

Overcoming Guilt and Shame Around Sexuality

As Black women, they often carry the weight of society's expectations and judgments when it comes to their sexuality. The deeply ingrained stereotypes and stigmas surrounding Black women's sexuality can lead to feelings of guilt and shame that impact their ability to fully embrace and express themselves in this aspect of their lives.

It is important to acknowledge and address these feelings of guilt and shame in order to reclaim your sexual agency and autonomy. One way to do this is by recognizing the sources of these negative emotions. Whether they stem from societal norms, religious beliefs, past experiences, or interpersonal relationships, understanding where these feelings come from can help you challenge and dismantle them.

Healing from guilt and shame around sexuality requires self-compassion and self-forgiveness. It is essential to treat yourselves with kindness and understanding, acknowledging that you are not defined by your past mistakes or experiences. By practicing self-love and acceptance, you can begin to release the burden of guilt and shame and embrace your sexuality with confidence and joy.

Seeking support from trusted friends, family members, or mental health professionals can also be beneficial in overcoming feelings of guilt and shame. Opening up about your struggles with sexuality and receiving validation and encouragement can help you feel less alone and more empowered to embrace your authentic self.

Ultimately, overcoming guilt and shame around sexuality is a transformative journey towards self-discovery and self-acceptance. By confronting and challenging the negative narratives that have been imposed on you, you can reclaim your sexual autonomy and celebrate the beauty and power of your own desires and expressions. It is through this process that you can truly embrace and honor your sexuality as a Black woman, free from the constraints of societal judgment and shame.

Delving deeper into your own desires and understanding the complex intersectionality of your identity as a Black woman can lead to a profound sense of empowerment and liberation. Embracing your sexuality is not only an act of self-love but also a radical act of resistance against the oppressive systems that seek to control and diminish black women.

Through this journey of self-discovery and healing, you can forge a new path towards sexual liberation and authenticity. By owning your desires, embracing your sensuality, and rejecting the shame imposed upon you, you can rewrite the narrative of Black women's sexuality and reclaim your right to pleasure and fulfillment.

In the face of societal pressures and expectations, you can stand strong in your truth and refuse to be silenced or shamed. Your sexuality is a sacred and integral part of who you are, deserving of honor, respect, and celebration. As a Black woman, you can continue to break free from the chains of guilt and shame, stepping into your power and embracing the fullness of your sexual self with unapologetic pride.

Celebrating Your Femininity

As a woman, embracing and celebrating your femininity is a transformative journey of self-discovery and empowerment. It is a profound act of reclaiming and honoring your true essence as a woman in all its complexity and beauty.

Femininity is a multifaceted and dynamic expression of identity that transcends societal expectations and stereotypes. It is not limited to one particular set of qualities but encompasses a diverse range of strengths: from nurturing and empathetic to assertive and courageous. Embracing your femininity means embracing all these aspects of yourself with authenticity and confidence, without seeking validation or approval from external sources.

At the core of celebrating your femininity is the recognition and acceptance of your body as a sacred vessel of life and experience. In a world that often seeks to objectify and commodify women's bodies, embracing your physical self is a radical act of self-love and self-acceptance. It means reclaiming ownership of your body and treating it with the respect and care it deserves, free from the constraints of societal beauty standards and expectations.

Furthermore, celebrating your femininity means honoring your emotional depth and intuition as sources of strength and guidance. As a black woman, you are often discouraged from expressing your emotions openly and embracing your intuitive wisdom. However, embracing your femininity involves valuing your emotional intelligence and trusting your inner knowing as powerful tools for navigating life's complexities with grace and authenticity.

Celebrating your femininity also entails recognizing and amplifying the voices and stories of women throughout history and in contemporary society. It involves acknowledging the resilience and achievements of women in various fields and advocating for gender equality and social justice. By standing in solidarity with other women and uplifting each other's voices, we create a powerful collective force for positive change and empowerment.

Ultimately, embracing and celebrating your femininity is a transformative and liberating process of self-discovery and self-empowerment. It is about embracing all aspects of yourself as a woman – your strengths, vulnerabilities, and unique qualities – with pride and self-assurance. By living authentically and unapologetically in alignment with your true self, you not only empower yourself but also inspire others to do the same, creating a ripple effect of positive change and empowerment in the world.

Navigating Relationships and Sex

In this section, we will delve into the complexities of navigating relationships and sex as a black woman with a focus on communication, agency, and empowerment. As a black woman, you bring a unique intersectional perspective to the table when it comes to intimate relationships and sexuality.

Communication is the foundation of any healthy relationship, and it is especially crucial when discussing desires, boundaries, and expectations around sex as a black woman. Clear and open dialogue with your partner can help foster trust, understanding, and mutual respect in your relationship. It's important to prioritize your own needs and boundaries while also considering those of your partner.

Societal stereotypes and expectations can greatly influence how black women navigate their sexuality. It's essential to remember that your sexuality is your own, and you have the agency to define it on your terms. Embrace your sexuality with confidence and authenticity, free from external pressures or judgments. Celebrate the beauty and diversity of black womanhood in all its forms.

Trusting your instincts and intuition is key when exploring sexual activities and relationships. If something feels uncomfortable or crosses your boundaries, it's important to speak up and advocate for yourself. Your body and your choices belong to you, and it's crucial to prioritize your well-being and safety in all intimate interactions.

Self-love and self-care are essential practices for maintaining healthy relationships. Take the time to nurture your mental, emotional, and physical well-being, and don't hesitate to seek support from loved ones or professionals when needed. Remember that your worth is not defined by your relationships or sexual experiences, but by the love and respect you show to yourself.

Embrace your unique journey as a black woman navigating relationships and sex, honoring your authentic self and valuing your worth. Cultivate relationships that uplift and support you, and continue to explore love and self-discovery with courage and empowerment. Your voice, your desires, and your boundaries matter, and they deserve to be respected and honored in all aspects of your life.

Empowering Black Women in Their Sexual Journey

In this profound exploration of the unique experiences and challenges faced by Black women in their sexual journey, lets delve deeper into the multifaceted layers of history, identity, and empowerment that shape their perspectives and interactions with their own sexuality.

The historical context of racist depictions and stereotypes that have long pervaded society's understanding of Black women's sexuality cannot be overlooked. From the dehumanizing narratives of hypersexuality to the objectification and fetishization of Black bodies, these damaging portrayals have not only marginalized but also distorted the true essence of Black women's sexual identities. By acknowledging and confronting these harmful stereotypes, Black women can begin to reclaim their agency and redefine their sexual narratives on their own terms.

Intersectionality emerges as a critical lens through which to view Black women's experiences with sexuality. The confluence of race, gender, and other intersecting identities informs and shapes how Black women navigate relationships, intimacy, and self-perception. It is essential to recognize and honor the unique complexities and nuances that arise at the intersection of these identities, as they influence how Black women determine their own desires, boundaries, and autonomy in their sexual lives.

Empowerment emerges as a central theme in this extended exploration, urging Black women to cultivate a deep sense of self-worth and confidence in their sexual expression. By embracing their heritage, culture, and beauty, Black women can find strength and liberation in honoring their authentic selves. Through acts of self-love, self-care, and self-advocacy, Black women can dismantle oppressive systems and reclaim ownership of their bodies and desires.

Community support and solidarity play a crucial role in fostering a sense of belonging and empowerment among Black women. By engaging in open and honest conversations, sharing experiences, and uplifting one another, Black women can create safe spaces where they feel seen, heard, and valued. In nurturing relationships built on trust, respect, and understanding, Black women can cultivate a culture of sisterhood that empowers them to navigate their sexual journeys with courage and resilience.

In conclusion, this extended chapter celebrates the resilience, beauty, and power of Black women as they navigate the intricate terrain of their sexuality. By embracing their identities authentically and challenging societal norms unapologetically, Black women can embark on a transformative journey of self-discovery and empowerment that transcends limitations and fosters a profound sense of joy and liberation.

This extended exploration underscores the importance of acknowledging the historical legacies of trauma and oppression that continue to impact Black women's sexuality today. By recognizing the ways in which systems of power and privilege shape our understandings of sexuality, we can begin to unravel the complexities and injustices that influence how Black women perceive and navigate their own desires and pleasures.

Furthermore, this conversation highlights the significance of centering pleasure and joy in discussions of Black women's sexuality. Too often, Black women's sexual experiences are framed within narratives of pain, trauma, and struggle, reinforcing harmful stereotypes and erasing the beauty and depth of their intimate connections. By prioritizing pleasure as a key aspect of sexual empowerment, Black women can reclaim agency over their bodies and redefine their relationships with sensuality and eroticism on their own terms.

Moreover, this extended exploration emphasizes the importance of holistic approaches to sexual health and wellness within the Black community. By recognizing the intersections of physical, emotional, and spiritual well-being, Black women can cultivate a more nuanced understanding of their sexual selves and advocate for comprehensive resources and support that address their unique needs and experiences. Through initiatives that promote sexual education, access to healthcare, and discussions on pleasure and consent, Black women can nurture healthier and more fulfilling relationships with their bodies and desires.

Ultimately, this serves as a testament to the resilience, creativity, and power of Black women as they navigate the complexities of their sexual journey. By embracing their histories, claiming their pleasures, and fostering inclusive communities of support and affirmation, Black women can embark on a transformative path towards sexual liberation and self-fulfillment that celebrates their innate beauty, strength, and authenticity.

Exercise is really important to me - it's therapeutic. So, if I'm ever feeling tense or stressed or like I'm about to have a meltdown, I'll put on my iPod and head to the gym or out on a bike ride along Lake Michigan with the girls.
— Michelle Obama

CHAPTER 7

Creating Dynamic Health

Embracing Your Health Journey

As you embark on your health journey, it is imperative to delve into the intricate web of factors that contribute to a holistic approach to well-being. Understanding the interconnectedness of physical, mental, emotional, social, environmental, and spiritual health allows for a more profound exploration of how these elements interact to shape our overall wellness.

Physical health, the foundation of our well-being, encompasses more than just the absence of illness. It is about nurturing our bodies through proper nutrition, regular exercise, adequate rest, and proactive healthcare. A balanced diet rich in nutrients, engaging in physical activities that bring joy and vitality, prioritizing quality sleep to allow for restoration and healing, and staying informed about preventive health measures are all vital components of supporting optimal physical health.

Mental health, often intertwined with emotional well-being, is a complex tapestry of our thoughts, feelings, and behaviors. Managing stress, practicing mindfulness, cultivating self-awareness, and developing healthy coping strategies are essential aspects of nurturing our mental health. Building resilience to navigate life's challenges, fostering meaningful relationships that provide support and connection, and engaging in activities that enhance cognitive function and emotional regulation all play a role in maintaining mental well-being.

Emotional health involves developing a deep understanding and acceptance of our emotions, allowing us to experience and express them authentically. This includes practicing self-compassion, managing challenging emotions effectively, and cultivating a strong sense of emotional intelligence. Building emotional resilience through adversity, engaging in practices that promote emotional regulation and self-awareness, and seeking professional support when needed are key components of nurturing emotional well-being.

Social health underscores the importance of strong and supportive relationships in our lives. Building meaningful connections, fostering a sense of belonging and community, and engaging in positive social interactions contribute to our overall well-being. Creating boundaries in relationships, seeking out social support during times of need, and nurturing healthy communication skills are all crucial aspects of supporting social health.

Environmental health acknowledges the impact of our surroundings on our well-being. Creating a safe, clean, and sustainable living environment, minimizing exposure to toxins, and connecting with nature to promote relaxation and rejuvenation are all ways to support environmental health. Embracing sustainable practices, being mindful of our ecological footprint, and advocating for environmental conservation can also contribute to our overall well-being.

Spiritual health, often rooted in a sense of purpose, meaning, and connection to something greater than ourselves, plays a significant role in our well-being. Engaging in practices that nourish the soul, such as meditation, prayer, mindfulness, or time spent in nature, can cultivate a sense of inner peace and fulfillment. Reflecting on our values, beliefs, and life purpose, and aligning our actions with our inner truth can support spiritual well-being.

By embracing a holistic view of health that considers the interconnected nature of physical, mental, emotional, social, environmental, and spiritual well-being, we can craft a comprehensive roadmap for living a more fulfilling and balanced life. Remember that your health journey is a continual process of self-discovery, growth, and self-care. Seek support and guidance along the way, and honor the unique path that leads to your optimal well-being.

Setting Realistic Goals

Setting realistic goals is the bedrock upon which any successful health and wellness journey is built. The process of goal-setting should be thoughtful, intentional, and tailored to your individual needs and aspirations. By establishing clear and attainable objectives, you equip yourself with a roadmap for progress and growth.

One effective strategy for setting realistic goals is to adhere to the SMART criteria - Specific, Measurable, Achievable, Relevant, and Time-bound. When a goal is specific, it specifies precisely what is to be accomplished, leaving no room for ambiguity. Measurable goals enable you to track your progress and stay accountable throughout your journey. An achievable goal is realistic and within reach, taking into account your current circumstances and resources. Concurrently, relevance ensures that your goals align with your values and aspirations, providing you with the motivation needed to stay committed. Finally, a time-bound goal establishes a clear endpoint, giving you a sense of urgency and direction.

Breaking down larger goals into smaller, digestible steps can help prevent feelings of overwhelm and boost your confidence as you progress. By celebrating each milestone, no matter how small, you reinforce positive habits and maintain momentum towards your ultimate objectives. Moreover, remaining flexible and adaptive in your goal-setting allows you to pivot and adjust as needed, accommodating for unforeseen challenges or changes in circumstances.

Recognizing that setbacks are a normal part of any journey is essential. Instead of viewing setbacks as failures, see them as learning opportunities that can provide valuable insights and propel you forward. Embrace resilience and perseverance in the face of adversity, knowing that setbacks do not define your ultimate success.

Moreover, understanding your intrinsic motivation behind your goals can significantly impact your commitment and perseverance. Reflecting on why a particular goal is important to you can deepen your sense of purpose and drive, making it easier to stay focused and dedicated, even in challenging times. Aligning your goals with your core values and aspirations can create a meaningful connection that sustains your motivation over the long term.

Additionally, involving others in your goal-setting process can provide invaluable support and accountability. Sharing your goals with a trusted friend, family member, or mentor can help keep you on track, provide encouragement when needed, and celebrate your achievements along the way. Building a supportive community around your goals can create a sense of camaraderie and shared commitment, making the journey towards wellness more enjoyable and fulfilling.

In essence, setting realistic goals is not just about the destination but the journey itself. It is about the growth, self-discovery, and resilience that you cultivate along the way. By approaching goal-setting with intention, mindfulness, and self-compassion, you lay the groundwork for sustainable and transformative change in your health and well-being.

Mindful Eating for Optimal Health

In today's modern society, where distractions are abundant and schedules are demanding, the simple act of eating has often become a rushed and mindless activity for many. Amidst the chaos of daily life lies an ancient practice that offers a path to greater health and well-being: mindful eating.

At its core, mindful eating is a profound practice that invites us to engage fully with the present moment, embracing the sensory experience of food with awareness and gratitude. By slowing down and tuning into our body's cues, we can cultivate a deeper connection to our food and ourselves, fostering a more balanced and harmonious relationship with what we eat.

When we approach our meals mindfully, we are invited to savor each bite, observing the colors, textures, and flavors of the food before us. Taking the time to chew slowly and deliberately, we can fully appreciate the nourishment that sustains us and the intricate symphony of sensations that come with each mouthful.

But mindful eating is not just about the physical act of consuming food—it is also a practice of heightened awareness and self-discovery. By tuning into our body's hunger and fullness signals, we can learn to trust our inner wisdom and respond to our needs more intuitively, rather than being driven by external influences or emotional triggers.

Furthermore, mindful eating offers us a window into our emotional and mental states, illuminating the ways in which our feelings and thoughts can impact our relationship with food. Through mindful awareness, we can begin to recognize patterns of emotional eating, stress-induced cravings, or mindless snacking, and develop healthier ways of coping with our emotions and nourishing our bodies.

Moreover, the practice of mindful eating can lead to a deeper understanding of our interconnectedness with the wider world. When we approach our meals with mindfulness, we are not just consuming food; we are partaking in a profound act of communion with the earth, the farmers who grew the produce, and the hands that prepared the meal. This awareness can foster a sense of gratitude and respect for the interconnected web of life that sustains us, encouraging us to make more conscious and sustainable choices in our food consumption.

Ultimately, the practice of mindful eating is a journey of self-discovery and self-care—a journey that invites us to slow down, listen deeply, and savor the richness of each moment at the table. By embracing mindfulness in our eating habits, we can cultivate a greater sense of presence, gratitude, and balance in our lives, nourishing not only our bodies but also our souls.

The Power of Regular Exercise

Regular exercise is a cornerstone of overall health and well-being, playing a crucial role in maintaining physical, mental, and emotional balance. The benefits of regular physical activity extend far beyond just keeping the body in shape; they encompass a holistic approach to health that can enhance every aspect of our lives.

From a physical perspective, engaging in regular exercise is essential for optimizing cardiovascular health, strengthening muscles and bones, and improving flexibility and mobility. Consistent physical activity also contributes to maintaining a healthy weight, reducing the risk of obesity and associated health conditions. The impact of exercise on our physical health extends to our internal systems as well, with improved circulation, enhanced lung capacity, and better digestion being among its many benefits. Furthermore, regular exercise can play a key role in managing chronic conditions such as hypertension, diabetes, and arthritis, helping individuals lead healthier and more active lives.

In addition to the physical benefits, exercise is also a powerful tool for promoting mental health and emotional well-being. Physical activity has been shown to release endorphins, neurotransmitters that act as natural mood enhancers, helping to alleviate symptoms of stress, anxiety, and depression. The mental benefits of exercise go beyond mood regulation, extending to improved sleep quality, heightened cognitive functions, and enhanced psychological well-being. Engaging in physical activity can provide a sense of accomplishment, boost self-esteem, and foster a positive outlook on life, contributing to overall mental wellness.

Moreover, exercise is a valuable tool for fostering social connections and building a sense of community. Group fitness classes, team sports, or exercise buddies can provide accountability, motivation, and a sense of camaraderie, enhancing the overall exercise experience. The communal aspect of physical activity can lead to increased social interaction, decreased feelings of isolation, and a support system that encourages and reinforces healthy habits. The emotional benefits of exercising in a group setting can amplify the positive effects on mental health, creating a synergistic relationship between physical activity and emotional well-being.

Finding a form of exercise that brings joy and satisfaction is key to establishing a sustainable routine. Whether it's through group fitness classes, outdoor activities like hiking or cycling, or solo practices like yoga or running, incorporating activities that resonate with your interests and preferences can make exercise a rewarding and fulfilling experience. Consistency is essential when it comes to reaping the full benefits of exercise, so finding a schedule that works for you and fits into your daily routine is crucial for long-term success.

Ultimately, prioritizing regular exercise is an investment in your overall well-being. By making physical activity a non-negotiable part of your lifestyle, you are nurturing your body, mind, and spirit in a way that promotes health, vitality, and longevity. Embrace the transformative power of regular exercise as a foundation for a balanced and fulfilling life.

Finding Joy in Movement

As you embark on your health journey, finding joy in movement can be a powerful and fulfilling experience. Movement is not just about burning calories or achieving a certain physique; it's a profound way to connect with your body on a deeper level and discover the limitless potential it holds.

One of the key aspects of finding joy in movement is exploring a variety of activities to discover what resonates with you. From the flowing movements of yoga to the exhilarating rush of dancing, the world of physical activity is vast and diverse. By trying out different forms of exercise, you can tap into your innate curiosity and uncover hidden passions that bring you alive.

Physical activity has been shown to have numerous benefits for both body and mind. Regular exercise can improve cardiovascular health, boost mood, reduce stress, and increase energy levels. Engaging in physical movement also helps to strengthen muscles, improve flexibility, and enhance overall physical fitness. The benefits of movement extend beyond the physical realm; they can also have a profound impact on mental health and emotional well-being.

In addition to exploring new activities, it's essential to listen to your body and honor its needs throughout your movement journey. Pay attention to how different exercises make you feel physically, emotionally, and mentally. Your body is constantly sending you messages, and tuning in to these signals can help you tailor your movement practice to suit your unique needs and preferences.

Mindful movement is a powerful practice that involves being fully present and aware during physical activity. By focusing on the sensation of each movement, the rhythm of your breath, and the alignment of your body, you can deepen your connection to yourself and the present moment. Mindful movement can cultivate a sense of calm, reduce anxiety, and enhance overall well-being.

Moreover, integrating movement into your daily life in a way that feels natural and sustainable is key to long-term success. Whether it's taking a brisk walk in nature, practicing gentle stretches in the morning, or engaging in playful movement with loved ones, finding ways to incorporate physical activity into your routine can enhance your overall well-being and joy.

Ultimately, finding joy in movement is a journey of self-discovery and self-love. It's about celebrating the incredible abilities of your body and reveling in the simple pleasure of moving through the world. By embracing movement as a form of self-expression and self-care, you can unlock a profound source of fulfillment and vitality that empowers you to live your best life.

Nurturing Your Body with Self-Care

In a fast-paced world where self-care is often overlooked, it is important to prioritize nurturing your body and mind to maintain overall well-being. Self-care is not selfish; it is a vital part of maintaining a healthy and balanced lifestyle.

Self-care encompasses a wide range of practices that are essential for cultivating self-love and self-compassion. It involves tuning into your physical, emotional, and mental needs to ensure that you are taking care of yourself in a holistic manner. Self-care is about creating a sustainable and nurturing relationship with yourself, acknowledging your worth and taking the time to replenish your energy reserves.

One fundamental aspect of self-care is maintaining a healthy lifestyle, which includes regular exercise, nutritious eating habits, and sufficient rest. Engaging in physical activity not only benefits your body but also has a positive impact on your mental well-being by releasing endorphins, the body's natural mood elevators. Exercise has been shown to reduce symptoms of anxiety and depression, improve cognitive function, and enhance overall quality of life.

Eating a balanced diet rich in fruits, vegetables, whole grains, and lean proteins provides your body with the necessary nutrients to function optimally and support your overall health. Proper nutrition is essential for maintaining a strong immune system, reducing the risk of chronic diseases, and supporting physical and mental well-being. Hydrating your body with an adequate amount of water each day is also crucial for proper physiological functioning and overall health.

In addition to physical self-care, nurturing your emotional and mental well-being is crucial for maintaining a healthy balance. This can include practices such as mindfulness meditation, journaling, or engaging in activities that bring you joy and fulfillment. Taking time to unwind and relax, whether through reading a book, listening to music, or spending time in nature, can help reduce stress and promote mental clarity.

Self-care is a personal journey, and it is essential to identify the practices that work best for you. It is not a one-size-fits-all approach but rather a tailored regimen that addresses your unique needs and preferences. By prioritizing self-care, you are investing in your long-term health and happiness, enhancing your ability to cope with life's challenges and fostering a sense of inner peace and personal fulfillment. By taking care of yourself, you are better equipped to show up fully in all aspects of your life, nurturing your relationships, pursuing your goals, and living authentically.

Understanding the Importance of Rest

Rest is often overlooked in our fast-paced society, where productivity is emphasized and busyness is glorified. However, rest is a critical component of our overall health and well-being. It is during periods of rest that our bodies have the opportunity to recharge, repair, and rejuvenate.

Physically, rest is essential for allowing our muscles to recover and grow stronger after exercise. When we engage in physical activity, our muscles undergo micro-tears that need time to heal and rebuild. Without adequate rest, these muscles may not have the chance to repair themselves fully, leading to a higher risk of injury and decreased performance over time. Additionally, rest plays a crucial role in regulating our metabolism and promoting proper hormonal balance, both of which are essential for overall health.

Moreover, rest is vital for our immune system. During sleep, our bodies produce cytokines, proteins that help regulate immune responses and fight off infections. Chronic sleep deprivation can lower the production of these cytokines, weakening our body's ability to combat illness. By prioritizing rest and ensuring we get enough sleep each night, we can bolster our immune defenses and reduce the likelihood of falling ill.

Mentally, rest is crucial for reducing stress and improving cognitive function. When we are sleep-deprived or constantly pushing ourselves without breaks, our bodies release stress hormones like cortisol, which can have detrimental effects on our mental health. Chronic stress has been linked to a range of mental health issues, including anxiety and depression. Taking time to rest, relax, and engage in activities that promote mental well-being, such as mindfulness or meditation, can help us maintain emotional resilience and cope better with life's challenges.

Emotionally, rest provides us with the space to process our thoughts and feelings. In today's fast-paced world, it is easy to become overwhelmed by the constant flow of information and stimuli. By intentionally carving out time for rest and relaxation, we give ourselves the opportunity to step back, reflect on our experiences, and reconnect with our inner selves. This introspective process can deepen our self-awareness, enhance our emotional intelligence, and promote a sense of inner peace and contentment.

In a culture that often values productivity over self-care, it can be challenging to prioritize rest. However, it is important to recognize that rest is not a sign of weakness or laziness, but rather a necessary part of maintaining our health and vitality. By honoring our need for rest and finding ways to incorporate it into our daily routines, we can support our overall well-being and live more fulfilling lives.

Furthermore, research has shown that restorative rest can have long-lasting effects on our cognitive abilities and creativity. When we are well-rested, our brains are better equipped to consolidate memories, make connections between different pieces of information, and think creatively. This is why taking breaks during intense periods of work or study can actually improve our overall performance and productivity in the long run. By allowing our minds the time and space to rest, we give ourselves the opportunity to approach problems from new perspectives and come up with innovative solutions.

On a spiritual level, rest can also be a powerful tool for self-discovery and inner growth. In moments of quiet contemplation and relaxation, we can tap into our inner wisdom and intuition, gaining insights into our true desires and values. By listening to the whispers of our soul during moments of rest, we can align our actions and choices with our deepest aspirations, leading to a more authentic and fulfilling life.

In essence, rest is not just a physical necessity but a holistic practice that encompasses our physical, mental, emotional, and spiritual well-being. By embracing rest as a vital part of our daily routine, we can nurture all aspects of ourselves and cultivate a greater sense of balance, joy, and fulfillment in our lives. Let us remember that true productivity and success are not measured solely by our output but by the quality of our presence, connection, and inner peace that we bring to each moment.

Cultivating a Positive Mindset

In today's fast-paced and often chaotic world, it can be all too easy to get swept up in negative thoughts and emotions that cloud our judgment and stifle our happiness. However, the power of positivity cannot be underestimated in its ability to transform our lives for the better. Cultivating a positive mindset is not just a feel-good cliché; it is a fundamental practice that can enhance our overall well-being, relationships, and even our success in various aspects of life.

One of the most potent practices for fostering positivity is the act of gratitude. Taking a few moments each day to reflect on the blessings in our lives can shift our focus from what is lacking to what is abundant. Whether it's the warmth of the sun on our skin, the laughter of our loved ones, or the simple pleasure of a warm cup of tea, expressing gratitude can anchor us in the present moment and remind us of the beauty that surrounds us.

Challenging negative thoughts is another crucial step in cultivating a positive mindset. Our minds have a tendency to latch onto negativity, feeding us distorted perceptions of reality that can snowball into anxiety and despair. By questioning these negative beliefs and looking for more balanced perspectives, we can start to unravel the grip they have on our minds and hearts. This practice of cognitive restructuring can help us see challenges as opportunities for growth and setbacks as temporary roadblocks on the path to success.

Surrounding ourselves with positivity is essential for sustaining a positive mindset. Our environment and the people we interact with can profoundly impact our mood and outlook on life. Seek out friendships that uplift and inspire you, engage with art, music, and literature that nourish your soul, and create spaces that evoke feelings of joy and peace. By intentionally curating a positive environment, we can better support our efforts to maintain a sunny disposition.

Practicing self-compassion is a vital component of cultivating positivity. Too often, we are our harshest critics, quick to judge ourselves for perceived flaws and failures. Embracing self-compassion means treating ourselves with the same kindness and understanding that we would offer to a dear friend in need. By acknowledging our humanity, mistakes, and imperfections with gentleness and empathy, we can foster a sense of inner peace and self-acceptance that lays the foundation for a positive mindset.

Focusing on solutions rather than dwelling on problems is a powerful mindset shift that can propel us forward in times of adversity. When faced with challenges, it can be tempting to succumb to despair and hopelessness. However, by adopting a problem-solving attitude and actively seeking out solutions, we can tap into our creative potential and resilience. Viewing obstacles as opportunities for growth and learning can empower us to navigate life's twists and turns with grace and determination.

Engaging in positive self-talk is a transformative practice that can boost our self-esteem and confidence. The way we speak to ourselves internally shapes our self-perception and influences our behavior. By replacing self-critical thoughts with positive affirmations and words of encouragement, we can rewire our brains to focus on our strengths and capabilities. Embracing a mindset of self-belief and empowerment can fuel our endeavors and help us overcome self-doubt and fear.

In conclusion, cultivating a positive mindset is a profound journey of self-discovery and growth. By incorporating practices such as gratitude, cognitive restructuring, self-compassion, solution-focused thinking, and positive self-talk into our daily lives, we can nurture a mindset of optimism, resilience, and joy. This intentional shift in perspective can ripple outwards, touching every aspect of our lives and creating a ripple effect of positivity that elevates not only ourselves but also those around us. Embrace the power of positivity and watch as it transforms your world in ways you never imagined possible.

Building a Supportive Community

In the intricate tapestry of life, the significance of cultivating a supportive community on the path to optimal health cannot be overstated. As we navigate the complexities of maintaining well-being in a fast-paced and often demanding world, the role of a nurturing, understanding, and encouraging community becomes paramount in our holistic journey towards health and wellness.

At the core of every thriving community are bonds forged through shared values and aspirations. By surrounding ourselves with individuals who align with our vision for health and wellness, we create a foundation of mutual understanding and camaraderie that serves as a source of inspiration and motivation. These like-minded companions not only empathize with our struggles but also celebrate our triumphs, fostering a sense of belonging and unity that bolsters our resolve to stay committed to our health goals.

In the heart of a supportive community lies the power of accountability. When we are held to a standard by those who genuinely care about our well-being, we are more likely to stay true to our commitments and follow through on our intentions. The gentle nudges and firm encouragements from our community members serve as gentle reminders of our priorities and responsibilities, urging us to remain steadfast in our journey towards a healthier lifestyle.

Furthermore, within the embrace of a nurturing community, we find a sanctuary for open and honest communication. The ability to share our vulnerabilities, challenges, and aspirations without fear of judgment or scrutiny fosters an environment of trust and understanding. Through these authentic exchanges, we not only deepen our connections with others but also gain invaluable insights and perspectives that propel our personal growth and self-awareness.

It is within the dynamics of a supportive community that we discover the transformative power of reciprocal support. As we receive encouragement and guidance from our fellow members, we are likewise called to uplift and empower others on their individual paths to well-being. This cycle of giving and receiving creates a harmonious flow of positive energy within the community, nurturing a culture of compassion, generosity, and resilience that propels each member towards their highest potential.

In conclusion, the journey towards optimal health is enriched and elevated by the presence of a supportive community. Through shared experiences, mutual encouragement, and genuine connections, we find the strength and inspiration to navigate the challenges and triumphs of our health journey with grace and determination. As we lean on and uplift each other within the embrace of a nurturing community, we create a tapestry of wellness that reflects the beauty and resilience of collective support in fostering a healthier, happier, and more fulfilling life.

Advocating for Your Own Health

In this section, we delve into the importance of advocating for your own health. Taking an active role in your healthcare journey is crucial for achieving optimal health outcomes. Advocating for yourself means being informed, asking questions, and actively participating in decision-making alongside your healthcare providers.

One key aspect of self-advocacy is being proactive about your health. This proactive approach involves not only seeking regular check-ups and following through with recommended screenings and tests but also taking a holistic view of your health. This includes being mindful of factors such as diet, exercise, stress levels, and mental health – all of which play a significant role in overall well-being. By adopting a proactive stance towards all aspects of your health, you can lay the foundation for lasting wellness.

Effective communication is another cornerstone of self-advocacy. Building a strong rapport with your healthcare providers involves not only expressing your concerns and symptoms but also actively listening to their expertise and advice. Remember that collaboration is key in the healthcare setting, and by fostering open, honest communication, you can ensure that your voice is heard and your healthcare needs are met.

Moreover, self-advocacy extends beyond the walls of the doctor's office. It involves being proactive in managing your health outside of formal healthcare settings. This may include making lifestyle changes to support your well-being, such as adopting a healthier diet, incorporating regular exercise into your routine, managing stress through mindfulness or relaxation techniques, and seeking out local resources or support groups for additional help and guidance.

Education is a powerful tool in self-advocacy. Take the time to research your health conditions, treatment options, and potential side effects. Seek out reliable sources of information, ask questions during medical appointments, and don't hesitate to request clarification on anything that feels unclear. By arming yourself with knowledge, you can make more informed decisions about your health and treatment plan.

Furthermore, seeking a second opinion or exploring alternative treatment options may be necessary parts of advocating for your health. Trusting your instincts and seeking out additional perspectives can provide valuable insights and help you feel more confident in the decisions you make regarding your health and well-being.

In conclusion, self-advocacy is a multifaceted approach that encompasses proactivity, communication, education, and empowerment. By taking an active role in your healthcare journey, you can optimize your health outcomes, foster a strong partnership with your healthcare providers, and ultimately work towards a healthier, more fulfilling life.

I did my best, and God did the rest.
— Hattie McDaniel

CHAPTER 8

Spirituality

Exploring the Differences Between Spirituality and Religion

When delving into the realms of spirituality and religion, it is essential to understand the distinctions between the two. While they are often intertwined and can complement each other, spirituality and religion present unique perspectives and practices that cater to different aspects of human experience.

Religion is typically structured around organized systems of beliefs, rituals, and practices that are shared by a community of followers. It often features established institutions, hierarchies, and doctrines that dictate the beliefs and behaviors of its adherents. Religion tends to provide a clear framework for understanding the divine, moral guidelines for living, and a sense of belonging to a community of believers.

On the other hand, spirituality is a more personal and individualistic approach to connecting with the divine or exploring the deeper aspects of existence. It is often characterized by a focus on inner experiences, intuition, and personal growth. Spirituality is about seeking meaning, purpose, and connection beyond the confines of traditional religious structures. It encourages individuals to explore their own beliefs, experiences, and values in pursuit of spiritual fulfillment.

While religion can offer a sense of belonging, tradition, and community, it can also be restrictive and dogmatic, stifling individual exploration and growth. Spirituality, on the other hand, provides freedom, flexibility, and a direct connection to one's inner truth, but it may lack the communal support and guidance found in religious communities.

It is important to recognize that spirituality and religion are not mutually exclusive, and many people find a balance between the two that suits their personal beliefs and needs. Some individuals derive spiritual inspiration and guidance from religious traditions, while others may choose to follow a more eclectic spiritual path that draws from various sources.

Moreover, spirituality often involves practices such as meditation, prayer, mindfulness, and contemplation, which are aimed at fostering a deeper connection with oneself, others, and the larger universe. These practices can cultivate a sense of inner peace, compassion, and harmony, leading to personal transformation and spiritual growth.

Religion, on the other hand, offers a structured approach to spirituality through established rituals, ceremonies, and communal worship. It provides a sense of continuity with traditions passed down through generations and offers a shared language and symbolism through which believers can connect with the divine and each other.

Ultimately, the exploration of spirituality and religion is a deeply personal journey that can lead to profound insights, transformation, and a deeper connection to oneself and the world around us. By understanding the differences between spirituality and religion, individuals can consciously choose the paths that resonate most with their beliefs, values, and aspirations.

Furthermore, spirituality is not limited to adherence to a specific dogma or creed; rather, it encompasses a broad spectrum of beliefs and practices that prioritize inner growth, mindfulness, and interconnectedness. Spirituality invites individuals to question, explore, and uncover their deepest truths and values, free from the constraints of rigid doctrines.

In contrast, religion often provides a sense of structure and clarity by offering a set of guidelines, rituals, and moral codes that govern the behavior and beliefs of its followers. This structure can be comforting and reassuring, as it establishes a sense of order and continuity in the midst of life's uncertainties.

However, the rigidity of religious dogma can also become a source of division, judgment, and exclusion, as individuals who do not conform to prescribed beliefs or practices may be marginalized or ostracized. This can lead to a sense of alienation and disillusionment among those who do not find themselves aligned with the teachings of a particular religion.

Spirituality, on the other hand, emphasizes personal experience, intuition, and inner wisdom as pathways to spiritual growth and fulfillment. It encourages individuals to delve deep into their own consciousness, cultivate mindfulness, and connect with the inherent interconnectedness of all beings. Spirituality is a journey of self-discovery, self-acceptance, and self-transformation that transcends the boundaries of religious institutions and dogmas.

In essence, spirituality and religion offer distinct approaches to the exploration of the divine and the mysteries of existence. While religion provides a structured framework for understanding and connecting with the divine, spirituality offers a more fluid and personalized path to inner growth, self-discovery, and interconnectedness with the world around us. Both spirituality and religion have the potential to enrich and inspire individuals on their spiritual journeys, offering unique perspectives and practices that resonate with different aspects of human experience.

The Importance of Connection to a Higher Power in a Black Woman's Life

In the hearts and souls of Black women, there exists a profound and intricate relationship with a higher power that transcends the constraints of time, culture, and circumstance, echoing throughout generations with a resonance that is both ancient and eternal. This divine connection, rooted in the rich tapestry of their history and experiences, serves as a guiding light that illuminates their path amidst the shadows of systemic oppression and societal marginalization.

Embedded within the fabric of their being, the spiritual bond between Black women and the divine is a wellspring of resilience, fortitude, and wisdom that sustains them through the trials and tribulations of life. It is a source of empowerment that empowers them to navigate the complexities of their identities with grace and authenticity, serving as a beacon of hope that shines brightly in the face of adversity.

From the harrowing days of slavery to the ongoing struggles against racism and sexism, Black women have drawn upon their faith and spirituality as a source of solace and strength, infusing their existence with a sense of purpose and meaning that transcends mere survival. In the quiet moments of prayer and meditation, they commune with their ancestors, whose spirits whisper words of encouragement and perseverance, reminding them of their inherent worth and resilience in the face of injustice.

The intersection of race, gender, and spirituality marks a sacred space where Black women's souls are nourished, their spirits uplifted, and their voices empowered to speak truth to power. It is within this sacred realm that they reclaim their agency, defiantly asserting their right to exist in all their beauty, complexity, and brilliance, unapologetically reaffirming their sacred place in the universe.

Through rituals and traditions passed down through generations, Black women honor the divine within themselves and each other, recognizing the interconnectedness of all beings and the sacredness of life itself. This spiritual kinship serves as a driving force that propels them forward on their journey towards self-discovery, self-love, and self-empowerment, forging a path towards a future where their light shines brightly and their voices resound with power and purpose.

In the profound depths of their souls, Black women's connection to a higher power is a testament to their resilience, their courage, and their unwavering belief in a greater good that transcends the limitations of the material world. It is a testament to their eternal spirit and indomitable strength, a testament to their enduring legacy of faith, hope, and love that binds them together in a sisterhood of divine grace and beauty.

Beyond the visible struggles they face, beyond the marginalization and oppression that seek to silence their voices, Black women find sanctuary in the arms of their spiritual beliefs. Their faith is not just a mere concept; it is the very essence that sustains them through the storms of life, anchoring them to a reality that goes beyond the physical realm.

Through their connection to the divine, Black women embody a sense of sacred purpose that infuses every aspect of their lives with meaning and significance. They walk with a quiet strength that stems from a deep knowing that they are divinely guided and protected, even in the face of adversity.

The rituals they perform, the prayers they recite, and the songs they sing are all expressions of their profound spiritual connection, weaving a tapestry of faith and resilience that has withstood the tests of time. In their communal gatherings and shared moments of worship, Black women find solace and solidarity, drawing strength from their collective bond with the divine and each other.

As they navigate the complexities of their identities and the challenges of their lived experiences, Black women draw upon the wellspring of their spirituality to find courage, wisdom, and inner peace.

Their faith is not passive; it is a source of active resistance against the forces that seek to diminish their worth and erase their contributions to the world.

In the sacred space of their souls, Black women honor the divine spark that resides within them, recognizing that they are the embodiment of a divine grace that transcends human understanding. They stand as pillars of strength and beacons of light, illuminating the path for others to follow in their footsteps of faith, resilience, and unwavering love.

Thus, the spiritual connection between Black women and the higher power is a testament to their enduring legacy of courage, grace, and dignity that continues to inspire and uplift generations to come. It is a sacred bond that weaves together the past, present, and future in a tapestry of divine love and eternal truth, reminding us all of the infinite possibilities that lie within the depths of our souls.

Breaking Free from Cultural and Familial Beliefs About God

Growing up in a traditional and conservative family, I was taught from a young age that there was only one way to believe in God. Our family's beliefs about God were deeply rooted in cultural and generational traditions that had been passed down for centuries. Questioning these beliefs was not encouraged, and any deviation from the accepted teachings was met with resistance and disapproval.

As I started to explore my own spirituality, I found myself grappling with conflicting emotions and thoughts. On one hand, I felt a deep sense of loyalty and obligation to uphold the beliefs that had been ingrained in me since childhood. On the other hand, I felt a strong pull to question and challenge these beliefs in search of my own truth.

Breaking free from cultural and familial beliefs about God was a daunting and challenging process. It meant confronting long-held assumptions and facing the possibility of disappointment and rejection from those closest to me. It meant stepping into the unknown and trusting in my own inner guidance and intuition.

But as I delved deeper into my exploration, I began to see the beauty and richness of embracing a more expansive and inclusive view of God. I realized that God was not confined to the narrow definitions and limitations that had been imposed upon me. God was vast and infinite, encompassing all beliefs and truths, welcoming diversity and individuality.

This journey of self-discovery led me to encounter a profound sense of interconnectedness with all beings and the natural world. I began to see that God was not an external force to be feared or appeased but a loving presence that permeated every aspect of existence. As I let go of rigid dogmas and embraced a more fluid understanding of spirituality, I felt a deep sense of peace and liberation within my soul.

Breaking free from cultural and familial beliefs about God was not just an act of rebellion; it was a sacred journey of reclaiming my true essence and aligning with my soul's purpose. Through this process of unlearning and relearning, I found a renewed sense of purpose and connection to something greater than myself.

In the end, this transformative experience allowed me to cultivate a more authentic and personal relationship with the divine. It taught me that God is not confined to the narrow constructs of human understanding but is an ever-evolving and infinite source of love and wisdom that transcends all boundaries. Breaking free from cultural and familial beliefs about God was a necessary and enlightening part of my spiritual evolution, guiding me towards greater authenticity, compassion, and unity with the universe.

Embracing Personal Truths and Inner Wisdom

In the profound journey of embracing personal truths and inner wisdom, we are confronted with the intricacies of our own being, where layers of conditioning and societal expectations have woven a web that obscures our most authentic selves. It is a journey that demands not only courage and self-reflection but also a radical commitment to excavating the depths of our soul in search of the truths that have long been buried beneath the surface.

As we navigate the labyrinthine corridors of our psyche, we come face to face with the shadows that dwell within us - the fears, insecurities, and unresolved traumas that have shaped our identities and influenced our perceptions of self. To embrace personal truths is to embark on a journey of reconciliation, where we must confront these shadows with compassion and humility, acknowledging their presence without allowing them to define us.

Simultaneously, the quest for inner wisdom beckons us to attune ourselves to the whispers of our soul - that timeless, eternal essence that transcends the confines of our physical existence. It is an invitation to cultivate a deep sense of presence and receptivity, to listen not only to the cacophony of external voices but also to the subtle, nuanced guidance that emerges from the depths of our being. In this sacred space of inner knowing, we discover a reservoir of wisdom that is both ancient and timeless, a wellspring of truth that flows from the source of our own divine nature.

As we weave together the threads of personal truths and inner wisdom, we begin to unravel the tapestry of our own existence, revealing patterns and connections that have long been obscured by the veils of illusion and misconception. It is a process of excavation and illumination, of shedding the layers of falsehood and pretense to reveal the radiant core of our being in all its resplendent beauty.

In embracing personal truths and inner wisdom, we are invited to embrace the full spectrum of our humanity - to honor our vulnerabilities and imperfections, our strengths and resilience, with a profound sense of self-acceptance and compassion. It is a journey that asks us to stand in our truth with unwavering courage and grace, to embody the essence of authenticity in a world that often demands conformity and uniformity.

As we tread the path of self-discovery and self-empowerment, may we find solace in the knowledge that the journey itself is the destination, and that in embracing our personal truths and inner wisdom, we rekindle the flame of our own divine essence, illuminating the path for others to follow in pursuit of their own inner light.

Unpacking the Fear-Based Theology in Organized Religion

In this section, we delve into the pervasive presence of fear-based theology within organized religion. From a young age, many individuals are taught to fear a higher power who punishes wrongdoing and rewards obedience. This fear is often instilled through stories of hell and damnation, creating a sense of guilt and shame for any perceived misdeeds.

Organized religions often use fear as a tool to control their followers, emphasizing the consequences of straying from the prescribed path. This fear-based approach can lead to a sense of unworthiness and separation from the divine, as individuals feel they must constantly measure up to impossible standards in order to avoid punishment.

However, as we explore the roots of fear-based theology, we begin to question its validity and impact on our spiritual journeys. Is it truly in alignment with the loving and compassionate nature of a higher power? Or is it a construct designed to maintain power and authority over believers?

Digging deeper into the origins of fear-based theology, we uncover how historical and cultural contexts have shaped these belief systems. Throughout centuries, fear has been used as a tool of manipulation and control by those in positions of authority within religious institutions. By invoking fear of punishment, these institutions have maintained influence and power over their followers, suppressing individual autonomy and critical thinking.

This reliance on fear as a driving force in religious teachings raises profound ethical and moral questions. Are fear-based narratives conducive to fostering genuine spirituality and moral growth, or do they inadvertently promote psychological harm and spiritual stagnation? The fear of punishment and eternal damnation can create a climate of anxiety and insecurity, leading individuals to prioritize compliance over personal growth and ethical reflection.

Moreover, the perpetuation of fear-based theology can contribute to division and intolerance within religious communities. When fear is utilized as a means of control, it can alienate those who question or challenge traditional doctrines, engendering a climate of judgment and exclusion rather than openness and acceptance. This rift within religious communities can hinder meaningful dialogue and collaboration, impeding the collective pursuit of spiritual enlightenment and ethical progress.

As we unravel the layers of fear-based theology, we start to recognize the importance of moving beyond fear and embracing a more loving and inclusive perspective of spirituality. By releasing the grip of fear, we can open ourselves up to a deeper connection with the divine that is based on love, acceptance, and inner peace. Through practices of compassion, forgiveness, and self-reflection, we can transcend fear and cultivate a spiritual journey grounded in authenticity and genuine connection with the higher power.

Cultivating a Love-Based Relationship with the Divine

In exploring the profound depths of cultivating a love-based relationship with the Divine, we are invited to immerse ourselves in the infinite sea of unconditional love that flows from the heart of the universe. This sacred journey beckons us to transcend the limitations of our human understanding and embrace the divine mysteries that unfold before us.

At the core of a love-based relationship with the Divine lies the recognition that love is the very fabric of creation itself. It is the cosmic force that sustains all life, the invisible thread that connects us to each other and to the divine source from which we have emerged. When we open ourselves to the boundless love of the Divine, we awaken to the truth that we are beloved children of the universe, cherished and held in the embrace of a love that knows no end.

This love-based spirituality is not merely a set of beliefs or rituals; it is a profound way of being and relating to the world around us. It calls us to move beyond the confines of our egoic self and into the realm of pure being, where we can experience the unity and interconnectedness of all things. In this state of expanded awareness, we come to understand that every act of kindness, every gesture of compassion, is a sacred offering to the Divine, a reverent expression of our deepest essence.

As we walk the path of love-based spirituality, we are invited to surrender our fears, doubts, and insecurities to the divine presence that dwells within us and around us. In the radiant light of love, we find solace for our burdens, healing for our wounds, and transformation for our souls. Through the practice of forgiveness, gratitude, and acceptance, we purify our hearts and cultivate a profound sense of inner peace that radiates outward, touching the lives of all whom we encounter.

In this sacred dance of love and grace, we discover that the Divine is not a distant deity to be feared or appeased but a loving presence that walks beside us, guiding us with wisdom and compassion. We learn to listen to the whispers of our soul, to heed the call of our inner truth, and to surrender to the divine will that flows through us and around us.

As we deepen our love-based relationship with the Divine, we come to realize that love is not just an emotion or a fleeting sentiment; it is the very essence of our being. It is the invisible force that animates our existence, the driving power that propels us toward our highest potential. In the embrace of divine love, we find the courage to confront our shadows, the strength to overcome our challenges, and the grace to shine our light into the world, inspiring others to do the same.

May we continue to walk this sacred path of love-based spirituality with open hearts and clear minds, knowing that we are held in the loving embrace of the Divine, now and for all eternity.

Finding Strength and Empowerment in Personal Spirituality

As individuals venture further into the realms of personal spirituality, they uncover a profound depth of wisdom and insight that transcends the limitations of the physical world. This sacred journey beckons them to explore the innermost recesses of their souls, unraveling the intricate tapestry of their being to reveal the essence of their true selves.

Within the sanctuary of personal spirituality, individuals confront the shadows that lurk within, those long-buried wounds and traumas that have shaped their perceptions and behaviors. Through acts of self-reflection and introspection, they embark on a path of healing and transformation, allowing light to penetrate the darkness and illuminate the path to wholeness.

The journey of personal spirituality is not merely a quest for empowerment but a reclamation of one's innate divinity and connection to the cosmic forces that animate the universe. It is a recognition of the sacredness that resides within each individual, a spark of the divine that yearns to be recognized and embraced.

By delving into the depths of their souls through contemplative practices and spiritual disciplines, individuals unearth a wellspring of inner strength and resilience that empowers them to navigate the complexities of existence with grace and fortitude. This inner fortitude serves as a beacon of light, guiding them through the tumultuous seas of life with unwavering faith and trust in the inherent goodness of the universe.

As individuals align with their spiritual essence, they begin to embody the virtues of compassion, empathy, and unconditional love, extending these qualities outwards to humanity and all living beings. This expansion of the heart fosters a deep sense of interconnectedness and unity, reminding individuals that they are integral threads in the fabric of creation, woven together in a tapestry of divine harmony.

Through the portal of personal spirituality, individuals transcend the confines of egoic identity and enter into a state of oneness with the cosmic dance of existence. They realize that they are not separate from the universe but intricately interwoven into its intricate web of life, pulsating with the same creative energy that births galaxies and stars.

This profound realization awakens within individuals a sense of purpose and meaning that transcends the mundane pursuits of material wealth and external validation. It ignites a fire within their souls, propelling them forward on a journey of self-discovery and self-realization, as they unfold the sacred blueprint of their destiny and contribute their unique gifts to the evolution of consciousness.

In the sanctum of personal spirituality, individuals find refuge and solace amidst the chaos and uncertainty of the world, drawing strength and inspiration from the wellspring of divine wisdom that flows through their hearts. They become beacons of light, illuminating the path for others to embark on their own journey of spiritual awakening and empowerment, recognizing that the true power lies not in external accolades or achievements but in the eternal flame of the soul that burns brightly within.

Honoring Ancestral Wisdom While Charting Your Own Spiritual Path

In the rich tapestry of our lives, the thread of ancestral wisdom runs deep, connecting us to our roots and guiding us on our spiritual journey. As Black women, they carry within them the stories and experiences of our ancestors, their struggles, triumphs, and resilience echoing through the generations.

Honoring ancestral wisdom is a profound act of reverence and acknowledgment of the path that has been paved for us. It is about recognizing the sacrifices made, the traditions passed down, and the knowledge preserved throughout the ages. Our ancestors held onto their faith and beliefs in the face of adversity, drawing strength from a source beyond themselves.

As we navigate the complexities of our spiritual paths, it is essential to understand that ancestral wisdom is not a one-size-fits-all approach. Each lineage carries its own distinct teachings, practices, and cultural contexts that shape the spiritual experiences of its descendants. By delving into our ancestral heritage, we gain a deeper understanding of who we are and where we come from, allowing us to weave together the tapestry of our identities with intention and reverence.

Ancestral wisdom is not confined to the past; it is a living, breathing force that continues to shape our present and future. By honoring our ancestors, we tap into a wellspring of knowledge and guidance that can help us navigate the challenges of our modern world with grace and resilience. Their voices whisper to us through the winds of time, reminding us of our inherent strength, resilience, and capacity for transformation.

In embracing the teachings of our ancestors, we also confront the shadows that linger within our lineage – the traumas, injustices, and struggles that have been passed down through generations. By shining a light on these darker aspects of our collective history, we can begin the work of healing and reconciliation, both within ourselves and our communities. Through this process of acknowledgment and healing, we pave the way for a brighter future, rooted in a deep sense of connection to our past.

As we honor our ancestors, we stand at the crossroads of tradition and innovation, drawing inspiration from the time-honored practices of our forebears while also forging our unique paths forward. It is a delicate dance of honoring the past while embracing the possibilities of the present and the visions of the future. In this sacred dance, we find ourselves held in a web of interconnectedness, our spiritual journeys intertwined with those who have come before us and those who will follow in our footsteps.

In the embrace of ancestral wisdom, we find not only a roadmap for navigating the complexities of our lives but also a wellspring of love, guidance, and support that transcends time and space. It is in this sacred space of connection and reverence that we discover the true depth of our identities and the eternal legacy of strength and resilience that flows through our veins.

Navigating Challenges and Criticisms on Your Journey to Truth

As you embark on your journey to discover your personal truth and deepen your spiritual connection, you are entering a realm of profound self-discovery and growth. This path you have chosen is one that holds the promise of inner wisdom, spiritual enlightenment, and a deeper understanding of the universe and your place within it. However, this journey is not without its challenges and criticisms, many of which can test your resolve and shake your foundation.

One of the most common challenges you may face on this spiritual path is the resistance and misunderstanding of those around you. People who do not share your beliefs may question your choices, dismiss your experiences, or even try to dissuade you from following your truth. It is important to remember that everyone's spiritual journey is unique, and what resonates with you may not necessarily resonate with others. Stay rooted in your convictions and trust in the guidance of your inner compass as you navigate through these external pressures.

Internal doubts and fears can also present themselves as formidable obstacles on your journey. As you delve deeper into spiritual truths and concepts that challenge your preconceived notions, you may find yourself grappling with uncertainty and self-doubt. Remember that growth often occurs outside of your comfort zone, and these moments of questioning are opportunities for introspection and personal transformation. Embrace the discomfort as a sign of growth and allow yourself the space to explore these uncertainties with an open heart and mind.

Criticism and judgment from others can be a harsh reality that you may encounter as you walk the path to truth. Individuals who do not understand or are threatened by your spiritual evolution may project their own insecurities onto you, leading to hurtful comments or dismissive attitudes. It is essential to cultivate a strong sense of self-worth and resilience in the face of external criticism. Remember, your worth and truth are not determined by the opinions of others, but by your own inner knowing and authenticity.

To navigate these challenges with grace and strength, seek support from like-minded individuals who understand and respect your journey. Engage in practices that nourish your spirit and provide you with a sense of grounding and clarity. Find solace in nature, meditation, or creative expression as ways to center yourself amidst the turmoil of external pressures.

Ultimately, the journey to truth is a deeply personal and transformative experience that only you can undertake. Trust in your intuition, honor your unique path, and stay committed to uncovering the depths of your inner wisdom. By navigating challenges and criticisms with resilience and self-assurance, you will emerge on the other side as a more empowered and enlightened version of yourself, ready to embrace the fullness of your truth and purpose in this vast and mysterious universe.

Embracing Freedom and Peace in Your Unique Spiritual Journey

As you journey on your path of personal spirituality, you may find that embracing freedom and peace is a deeply rewarding and transformative experience. This final section serves as a culmination of your growth and self-discovery, as you have navigated through the complexities of spirituality and religion to find your own truth.

Embracing freedom means letting go of constraints and expectations imposed by others or society. It is about breaking free from the fear-based teachings and embracing a love-based relationship with the Divine. By releasing outdated beliefs and dogmas, you open yourself up to new possibilities and deeper connections with your inner wisdom and higher power.

Finding peace in your unique spiritual journey involves accepting and honoring your truth, regardless of any external pressures or criticisms. It is about cultivating a sense of calmness and serenity within yourself, knowing that you are following the path that aligns with your authentic self and values. This inner peace provides a solid foundation for you to continue growing and evolving spiritually.

As you embrace freedom and peace in your spiritual journey, remember to stay open-minded and curious. Stay true to yourself, even in the face of challenges or doubts. Trust in your intuition and inner guidance, for they will lead you towards greater understanding and fulfillment.

May this section serve as a reminder that your spiritual journey is uniquely yours, and that finding freedom and peace within yourself is a constant process of self-discovery and growth. Embrace your journey with an open heart and a willingness to explore the depths of your soul, and you will find the freedom and peace you seek.

In this journey, you may also encounter moments of resistance or doubt from within and from external sources. It is essential to navigate these challenges with patience and self-compassion. Embrace the discomfort as an opportunity for growth and self-reflection, knowing that through these struggles, you will emerge stronger and more aligned with your true essence.

Remember that freedom and peace are not destinations to reach but ongoing states of being to cultivate. Be gentle with yourself as you continue to unfold the layers of your spirituality, acknowledging that growth is a nonlinear process with its own ebbs and flows. Trust in the wisdom of the universe to guide you along your path, and surrender to the beauty of the unknown with an open heart and mind.

As you embody freedom and peace in your spiritual journey, you radiate a light that inspires others to embark on their paths of self-discovery and spiritual growth. Embrace your role as a beacon of love and acceptance, inviting others to tap into their own inner power and wisdom. Together, we can create a world filled with compassion, understanding, and unity, rooted in the interconnectedness of all beings.

May your journey be blessed with freedom, peace, and a profound sense of purpose as you continue to walk your unique path of spiritual evolution. Trust in the divine orchestration of the universe and embrace the infinite possibilities that await you on this sacred journey of self-discovery and transformation.

When you allow yourself to release the shackles of fear and judgment, you create space for the boundless love and light of the universe to flow through you. In this space of freedom and peace, you can truly embody your highest self and live in alignment with your soul's purpose. Keep your heart and mind open to the infinite wisdom that surrounds you, and let the energy of love guide you on your spiritual journey towards greater depths of understanding and enlightenment.

Don't let anyone rob you of your imagination, your creativity, or your curiosity. It's your place in the world; it's your life. Go on and do all you can with it, and make it the life you want to live.
— Dr. Mae Jemison

CHAPTER 9

Get Your Mind Right To Get Your Money Right

Mindset Matters: How Your Beliefs Shape Your Money Reality

As we explore the profound impact of mindset on our financial journey, it becomes evident that our beliefs and attitudes towards money play a pivotal role in shaping our financial reality. These deep-seated beliefs are often ingrained in our subconscious minds and can either propel us towards wealth and success or hold us back in a cycle of scarcity and limitation.

Within the realm of mindset, the concept of money scripts comes into play. Money scripts are the unconscious, often inherited beliefs and attitudes we hold about money that influence our financial behaviors and decisions. These scripts are typically developed in childhood through observations of how money was handled by our caregivers and through societal messages about wealth and success.

Understanding and identifying our money scripts is crucial in unraveling the layers of our money mindset. By shining a light on these hidden beliefs, we can begin to challenge and reframe them, paving the way for a more empowered and abundant relationship with money.

One common money script that many individuals grapple with is the belief that money is scarce and hard to come by. This scarcity mindset can manifest in behaviors such as hoarding money, avoiding investments, or feeling anxious about financial decisions. By acknowledging and shifting this belief towards abundance and trust in the flow of resources, we can open ourselves up to greater financial opportunities and prosperity.

Furthermore, our mindset towards money is intricately linked to our self-worth and self-esteem. Many people tie their sense of worthiness to their financial status, leading to feelings of inadequacy or unworthiness if they do not meet certain financial benchmarks. Cultivating a healthy sense of self-worth independent of financial success is essential in fostering a positive money mindset and overall well-being.

Practicing mindfulness and self-awareness is key in cultivating a positive money mindset. By observing our thoughts and emotions around money without judgment, we can begin to unravel the layers of conditioning and limiting beliefs that may be holding us back. Mindfulness practices such as meditation, journaling, and gratitude exercises can help us rewire our brains for abundance and prosperity.

Our mindset towards money is a powerful force that shapes our financial reality. By delving deep into our money scripts, challenging limiting beliefs, and cultivating a positive relationship with money, we can pave the way for a more abundant, fulfilling, and prosperous life. It is through this journey of self-discovery and mindset transformation that we can unlock our true potential for financial success and well-being.

Unpacking Money Myths: Challenging Childhood Conditioning

It's important for us to delve further into the complex interplay of money myths that shape our beliefs and behaviors surrounding finances. Beyond the surface-level expressions and societal influences, there exist intricate layers of psychological and emotional conditioning that impact our relationship with money on a profound level.

Our childhood experiences with money are deeply ingrained in our subconscious minds, often influencing our financial habits and attitudes in ways we may not fully comprehend. Beyond the cliched sayings like "A penny saved is a penny earned," lie implicit messages about worthiness, safety, and security that shape our beliefs about abundance and scarcity.

The narratives we inherit about money from our families, communities, and cultures can be both empowering and limiting. The stories of struggle and sacrifice passed down through generations can instill a sense of duty or obligation around money, while societal norms and expectations can perpetuate harmful myths about success and wealth.

Moreover, the media plays a significant role in perpetuating money myths by portraying material wealth as a marker of status and happiness. These idealized images of prosperity can create unrealistic expectations and fuel feelings of inadequacy or comparison, leading to a distorted view of financial success.

Challenging these deeply ingrained beliefs requires courage and self-awareness. It entails questioning the stories we've been told about money and exploring the emotional triggers and fears that underpin our financial decisions. By shining a light on these hidden narratives, we can begin to unravel the unconscious patterns that govern our relationship with money.

Replacing these limiting money myths with empowering truths is a journey of personal growth and transformation. It involves reprogramming our mindset to see money as a tool for creating positive change in our lives and the world around us. By adopting a mindset of abundance and gratitude, we can cultivate a sense of financial freedom and empowerment that transcends traditional notions of wealth and success.

In essence, the exploration of money myths is a journey inward—a path of self-discovery and empowerment that leads us toward a more conscious and intentional relationship with money. By untangling the webs of conditioning and challenging the narratives that no longer serve us, we can pave the way for a new story—one grounded in abundance, purpose, and fulfillment in all aspects of our financial lives.

Think and Grow Rich Revisited: Harnessing the Power of Your Thoughts

An excellent resource to support you in changing your mindset about money is Napoleon Hill's classic book, "Think and Grow Rich,". It explores how the power of our thoughts can shape our financial reality. Hill's principle of "thoughts are things" underscores the importance of our mental outlook on wealth creation.

By understanding that our thoughts have the power to manifest our desires, we can begin to consciously direct our thoughts towards abundance and prosperity. Hill's concept of the Mastermind principle highlights the importance of surrounding ourselves with like-minded individuals who can support and elevate our financial goals.

Visualizing success and believing in our ability to achieve it are key aspects of harnessing the power of our thoughts. By aligning our thoughts, beliefs, and actions towards our financial goals, we can create a mindset that attracts wealth and opportunities into our lives.

Furthermore, the book emphasizes the importance of positive affirmations and the practice of affirming our financial goals daily. By consistently reinforcing our beliefs in our own financial success, we can reprogram our subconscious mind to support our wealth-building efforts.

Moreover, Hill also touches upon the concept of faith and persistence as crucial components in turning our thoughts into tangible wealth. Belief in ourselves and our ability to overcome obstacles is essential for staying committed to our financial goals over the long term.

Another key aspect highlighted in "Think and Grow Rich" is the idea of creating a definite plan for achieving our financial objectives. By setting clear, specific goals and taking consistent action towards them, we can harness the power of our thoughts to drive us towards success.

In addition to these principles, Hill emphasizes the importance of cultivating a burning desire for financial success. This intense passion and drive serve as the fuel that propels individuals towards their goals, even in the face of challenges and setbacks.

Furthermore, Hill stresses the role of specialized knowledge in the pursuit of wealth. By continuously expanding our knowledge and skills in a particular field, we can position ourselves as experts and increase our earning potential.

The concept of perseverance and resilience is also paramount in Hill's teachings. He highlights the importance of maintaining a positive attitude and bouncing back from failures, viewing them as opportunities for growth rather than setbacks.

Moreover, Hill emphasizes the significance of taking decisive action towards our financial goals. Simply thinking about wealth is not enough; we must translate our thoughts into tangible steps and consistently work towards achieving our objectives.

In conclusion, Napoleon Hill's insights from "Think and Grow Rich" underscore the transformative power of our thoughts in shaping our financial destiny. By aligning our mindset, beliefs, and actions towards abundance, surrounding ourselves with supportive individuals, affirming our goals, and taking persistent action, we can unleash our full potential for financial success and prosperity.

The Law of Attraction and Money: Manifesting Abundance

As we delve deeper into the intricacies of the Law of Attraction and its relationship to manifesting abundance, we uncover the profound connection between our thoughts, emotions, and vibrational energy. The Law of Attraction operates on the principle that everything in the universe is made up of energy, including our thoughts and emotions. When we focus our thoughts and feelings on a specific outcome, we emit a vibrational frequency that attracts similar energy back to us.

In the realm of finances and abundance, our beliefs about money play a crucial role in shaping our financial reality. The subconscious mind, which controls a significant part of our thoughts and behaviors, is deeply influenced by our beliefs and experiences surrounding money. If we hold onto limiting beliefs about money, such as "money is scarce" or "I will never be wealthy," we inadvertently create a barrier to attracting abundance into our lives. These deeply ingrained beliefs can create a cycle of scarcity and lack that keeps us from fully realizing our financial potential.

To shift our financial reality and align with the abundance we desire, it is essential to reprogram our beliefs about money. This can be done through various techniques such as affirmations, visualization, and hypnotherapy. Affirmations are powerful statements that affirm the reality we wish to create, such as "I am a magnet for wealth and abundance" or "Money flows to me easily and effortlessly." By repeatedly affirming these positive statements, we send new beliefs to our subconscious mind, gradually replacing old patterns of scarcity with a mindset of abundance.

Visualization is another potent tool in utilizing the Law of Attraction to manifest financial abundance. By creating detailed mental images of ourselves living a life of financial freedom, feeling the emotions of abundance, and truly believing in the reality of our vision, we activate the creative power of the mind. Visualization not only helps to clarify our desires but also strengthens our belief in the possibility of achieving them. When we can see and feel our financial goals as already accomplished, we align our energy with the frequency of abundance and signal to the universe that we are ready to receive.

Gratitude emerges as a fundamental practice in harnessing the Law of Attraction for financial abundance. By expressing heartfelt gratitude for the money, opportunities, and resources already present in our lives, we shift our focus from scarcity to abundance. Gratitude creates a positive energy flow that attracts more blessings and opportunities for wealth to flow into our lives. When we appreciate what we have, we open ourselves up to receiving even more abundance from the universe.

In addition to cultivating a positive mindset and practicing gratitude, taking inspired action is essential in manifesting financial abundance. The Law of Attraction responds to the energy and effort we put into pursuing our goals. By taking intentional steps towards increasing our income, savings, investments, or entrepreneurial endeavors, we align our physical actions with our desired financial outcomes and create a pathway for abundance to manifest in our lives. Inspired action could involve learning new skills, networking with potential collaborators, investing in personal development, or seizing opportunities that come our way.

In conclusion, the Law of Attraction serves as a powerful force for creating abundance and prosperity in our lives when we align our thoughts, emotions, and actions with our financial goals. By adopting a mindset of abundance, practicing gratitude, visualizing our desired outcomes, and taking inspired action, we unlock the limitless potential of the universe to bring wealth and abundance into our lives. Embrace the interplay between your thoughts, emotions, and actions, and watch as the Law of Attraction transforms your financial reality in ways beyond your imagination. Trust in the magnetic power of your thoughts and emotions to attract the wealth and abundance you seek, and know that you are the creator of your financial destiny.

Overcoming Scarcity Mentality: Cultivating an Abundance Mindset

In this in-depth exploration of scarcity mentality and abundance mindset, we delve deeper into the psychological and emotional factors that influence our perception of scarcity and abundance. Scarcity mentality is a deeply ingrained belief system that stems from a fear of lack and insufficiency. This fear can manifest in various areas of our lives, such as finances, relationships, and opportunities.

At its core, scarcity mentality is rooted in a sense of unworthiness and a belief that there are limited resources available to us. This mindset can lead to feelings of anxiety, competition, and a constant need to hoard and protect what little we have. The scarcity mindset operates from a place of fear, scarcity, and lack, causing us to focus on what we don't have rather than appreciating what we do possess.

Moreover, scarcity mentality often develops as a result of past experiences of deprivation or insecurity. For example, growing up in an environment where resources were scarce or feeling a sense of lack in childhood can deeply imprint a scarcity mindset that carries into adulthood.

These early experiences can shape our beliefs about the availability of opportunities and abundance in the world.

Conversely, an abundance mindset is characterized by a sense of gratitude, generosity, and confidence in the abundance of resources available to us. It involves shifting our perspective from scarcity and limitation to one of abundance and possibility. By cultivating an abundance mindset, we open ourselves up to a world of limitless opportunities, connections, and solutions.

One powerful way to shift from scarcity to abundance is through the practice of mindfulness. By being present in the moment and tuning into our thoughts and emotions, we can start to identify and challenge the scarcity-based beliefs that are holding us back. Mindfulness allows us to become aware of our thought patterns and choose more empowering and positive ways of thinking.

Furthermore, exploring the concept of abundance also involves acknowledging and appreciating the interconnectedness of all things. Recognizing that we are part of a vast web of relationships, resources, and energy can shift our perspective from one of individual lack to collective abundance. When we view ourselves as interconnected beings sharing in the collective wealth of the universe, we can tap into a profound sense of abundance that transcends material possessions.

Additionally, fostering a sense of gratitude and appreciation for the abundance in our lives can help rewire our brains to focus on the positive aspects of our existence. Gratitude is a powerful tool for shifting our mindset from lack to abundance, as it helps us see the inherent richness and blessings that surround us.

Ultimately, cultivating an abundance mindset is a continuous practice that requires self-awareness, intention, and a willingness to challenge our limiting beliefs. By embracing abundance in all areas of our lives and releasing the grip of scarcity mentality, we can create a life filled with richness, joy, and endless possibilities.

Money Blocks and Limiting Beliefs: Identifying and Breaking Through

In this section, lets delve into the deep-rooted money blocks and limiting beliefs that may be holding you back from achieving financial abundance. These beliefs are often formed in childhood or through past experiences, and they can have a powerful influence on your relationship with money.

Identifying these money blocks involves introspection and self-awareness. Reflect on your attitudes towards money, success, and wealth. Consider any recurring negative thoughts or emotions you have about money. Are there any patterns or beliefs that you notice cropping up consistently when it comes to finances? These could be signs of underlying money blocks.

Once you have identified your money blocks, the next step is to work on breaking through them. This process involves challenging and reframing your limiting beliefs. Replace negative thoughts with positive affirmations and empowering beliefs about money. Visualize yourself living a life of abundance and financial freedom. Practice gratitude for the money you have and focus on attracting more wealth into your life.

It's important to remember that breaking through money blocks is a journey, and it may take time and effort to shift your mindset. Be patient with yourself and stay committed to making positive changes. Seeking support from a coach or therapist can also be helpful in overcoming deep-seated money blocks.

By identifying and breaking through your money blocks and limiting beliefs, you can pave the way for a more prosperous and fulfilling financial future. Embrace the journey of self-discovery and empowerment as you work towards creating a new, abundant reality for yourself.

Furthermore, it's essential to recognize that money blocks can manifest in various forms, such as fear of success, fear of failure, or a scarcity mindset. These blocks can result in self-sabotaging behaviors, such as overspending, underearning, or avoiding financial opportunities. By addressing these underlying issues, you can create a more positive and healthy relationship with money.

One effective technique for overcoming money blocks is to practice mindfulness and self-awareness. Pay attention to your thoughts and emotions around money, and challenge any negative beliefs that arise. Cultivate a mindset of abundance and prosperity by focusing on gratitude, generosity, and positive thinking. Surround yourself with supportive and financially savvy individuals who can help you shift your perspective on money.

In addition to addressing internal money blocks, it's also important to examine external factors that may be contributing to financial limitations. This could include societal influences, cultural beliefs, or past experiences that have shaped your money mindset. By identifying and releasing these external influences, you can create a more empowered and liberated relationship with money.

Ultimately, breaking through money blocks requires a combination of self-reflection, mindset shifts, and supportive practices. By committing to this journey of growth and transformation, you can unlock your full potential for financial abundance and prosperity. Embrace the process with courage and determination, knowing that a wealthier and more fulfilling future awaits you on the other side of your money blocks.

Financial Self-Worth: Understanding Your Relationship with Money

In exploring the intricate dynamics of financial self-worth and its profound impact on our relationship with money, we unveil a complex interplay of psychological, societal, and personal factors that shape our financial behaviors and beliefs.

Financial self-worth, at its essence, is a reflection of our core beliefs about our deservingness of wealth, success, and prosperity. These beliefs are deeply ingrained from early childhood experiences, familial influences, cultural norms, and personal values, all of which contribute to our overall sense of worthiness in relation to financial abundance.

Individuals with a high degree of financial self-worth often exhibit traits of confidence, resilience, and a proactive mindset when it comes to managing their finances. They are more inclined to set ambitious monetary goals, take calculated risks, and view setbacks as opportunities for growth and learning. This positive self-perception not only influences their financial decisions but also spills over into other aspects of their lives, fostering a sense of empowerment and fulfillment.

Conversely, those grappling with low financial self-worth may find themselves trapped in a cycle of self-doubt, fear of scarcity, and a deep-rooted belief that they are undeserving of financial success. This mindset can manifest in behaviors such as overspending, avoiding financial planning, or settling for less than they deserve in terms of income and opportunities.

To cultivate a robust sense of financial self-worth, individuals are encouraged to engage in introspective practices that challenge and reshape limiting beliefs around money and self-value. This may involve seeking out financial education, practicing self-care, and surrounding oneself with a supportive network of mentors and peers who champion their financial growth.

Ultimately, cultivating a healthy sense of financial self-worth is a transformative journey that goes beyond mere monetary gains. It is about reclaiming one's inherent value, honing a mindset of abundance, and embracing the infinite possibilities that financial empowerment can bring to one's life. By engaging in intentional self-reflection and taking proactive steps to enhance our financial self-worth, we pave the way for a future brimming with prosperity, purpose, and self-assurance.

Creating a Money Mindset Practice: Daily Habits for Wealth

In this section, we delve even further into the profound impact of establishing a money mindset practice to truly transform your relationship with wealth and abundance. Cultivating a mindset that is aligned with prosperity is not just about positive affirmations and visualizations; it entails a holistic approach that encompasses deep-rooted beliefs and attitudes towards money.

Beyond the daily routines of affirmations and visualizations, it is crucial to explore and understand your core beliefs about money. These beliefs, often shaped by childhood experiences, societal conditioning, and past financial struggles, can either support or hinder your financial success. By uncovering and challenging limiting beliefs, you can reframe your mindset to one that is conducive to attracting wealth.

Moreover, integrating mindfulness practices into your money mindset routine can enhance your awareness of your financial habits and behaviors. Mindfulness allows you to observe your thoughts and emotions around money without judgment, enabling you to make conscious choices that align with your financial goals.

Setting clear and specific financial goals is another essential aspect of a robust money mindset practice. By defining your objectives, breaking them down into actionable steps, and regularly revisiting and adjusting your goals, you create a roadmap for financial success that keeps you motivated and focused.

Furthermore, practicing self-care and self-love as part of your money mindset practice can have a profound impact on your relationship with money. When you prioritize your well-being and cultivate a sense of worthiness and deservingness, you open yourself up to receiving abundance in all areas of your life, including finances.

In essence, developing a money mindset practice that goes beyond surface-level tactics to explore and transform your deep-seated beliefs, integrate mindfulness, set clear goals, and prioritize self-care is the cornerstone of creating lasting wealth and abundance. By embracing a holistic approach to cultivating a prosperous mindset, you pave the way for financial empowerment and fulfillment.

To deepen your understanding of money mindset, consider exploring the concept of abundance blocks – subconscious beliefs and thought patterns that can obstruct the flow of money into your life. By identifying and releasing these blocks through practices such as journaling, therapy, or energy work, you can clear the path for abundance to manifest effortlessly.

Additionally, reflecting on your money story – the narrative you tell yourself about your past, present, and future financial experiences – can offer valuable insights into your beliefs and attitudes towards money. By rewriting your money story from a place of empowerment and abundance, you can reshape your relationship with money and create a new narrative that aligns with your financial goals.

Furthermore, studying the principles of wealth consciousness and the law of attraction can enhance your money mindset practice by deepening your understanding of the energetic aspects of money. By raising your vibration and aligning your thoughts and emotions with abundance, you can attract wealth and prosperity into your life with greater ease and flow.

In conclusion, by delving deeper into the realms of abundance blocks, money stories, wealth consciousness, and the law of attraction, you can elevate your money mindset practice to new heights of awareness and transformation. Embracing these profound concepts and integrating them into your daily routine will not only shift your relationship with money but also open up new possibilities for creating a life of financial abundance and fulfillment.

Financial Goal Setting: Mapping Out Your Money Journey

As you embark on your financial journey, one of the most crucial steps you can take is to set clear and attainable financial goals. Goal setting is a powerful tool that can help you stay focused, motivated, and on track towards achieving financial success.

The first step in setting financial goals is to determine what you truly want to achieve with your money. Take some time to reflect on your values, priorities, and aspirations. Do you dream of buying a home, starting your own business, saving for your children's education, or traveling the world? Once you have a clear vision of your financial goals, you can begin to break them down into specific, measurable, achievable, relevant, and time-bound (SMART) objectives.

When setting financial goals, it's important to be realistic and consider your current financial situation. Assess your income, expenses, debts, savings, and investments to understand where you stand financially. From there, you can establish short-term, medium-term, and long-term financial goals that align with your circumstances and aspirations.

Create a budget that outlines how you will allocate your income towards achieving your financial goals. Identify areas where you can cut back on expenses and increase your savings. Consider automating your savings and investments to ensure consistent progress towards your goals.

Track your progress regularly and make adjustments as needed. Celebrate small wins along the way to stay motivated and focused on your financial goals. Remember that financial goal setting is a dynamic process that may require flexibility and adaptation as your circumstances change.

In addition to setting specific financial goals, it's important to consider the broader context of your financial well-being. Think about your overall financial health, including your emergency fund, insurance coverage, retirement planning, and estate planning. These aspects play a crucial role in your long-term financial stability and should be integrated into your goal-setting process.

Consider working with a financial advisor to help you refine your financial goals, develop a comprehensive financial plan, and navigate complex financial decisions. A professional can offer valuable insights, strategies, and guidance to support you in achieving your financial goals effectively and efficiently.

By taking a holistic approach to financial goal setting and incorporating various aspects of your financial well-being, you can lay a solid foundation for your financial future. Stay committed to your goals, stay informed about financial best practices, and continue learning and growing on your money journey. With dedication, planning, and a clear vision, you can build a secure and prosperous financial future for yourself and your loved ones.

Money Mastery: Thriving in Abundance

As you immerse yourself in the journey of mastering money, you begin to realize that true wealth encompasses far more than just financial abundance. Money mastery is a multifaceted concept that intertwines mindset, values, actions, and intentions to create a holistic sense of prosperity in all aspects of life.

At its core, mastering money involves cultivating a deep understanding of the relationship between your thoughts and beliefs regarding wealth and your tangible financial outcomes. Recognizing and addressing any limiting beliefs or scarcity mindsets is crucial in opening up to the flow of abundance that surrounds you. By shifting your perspective to one of sufficiency and possibility, you can tap into the boundless opportunities that await.

Gratitude plays a pivotal role in the journey towards money mastery, serving as a powerful magnet for further abundance. When you acknowledge and appreciate the blessings already present in your life, you open yourself up to receiving even more abundance in return. Gratitude acts as a transformative force, shifting your focus from what is lacking to what is already abundant, thereby amplifying your prosperity consciousness.

Setting clear and aligned financial goals is another integral component of money mastery. By defining your aspirations and breaking them down into actionable steps, you empower yourself to take purposeful strides towards financial freedom. Aligning your goals with your values and vision for the future ensures that your pursuit of wealth is meaningful and fulfilling, guiding you towards a life of purpose and prosperity.

As you navigate the complexities of the financial landscape, seeking mentorship and guidance from those who have achieved success in this realm can provide invaluable insights and support. Surrounding yourself with individuals who share your values and aspirations creates a supportive network that propels you towards your financial goals. Embracing a mindset of continuous learning and growth equips you with the skills and knowledge necessary to navigate challenges and seize opportunities along your journey.

In essence, money mastery is a profound journey of self-discovery and empowerment. It is a process of claiming your inherent worth and stepping into your role as a conscious creator of your financial destiny. By cultivating a mindset of abundance, setting aligned goals, and taking intentional action, you unlock the infinite possibilities that await you on the path to true wealth and prosperity.

The pursuit of money mastery also involves honing your financial literacy and understanding the various avenues through which wealth can be generated and preserved. Diversifying your income streams, investing wisely, and managing your assets effectively are essential strategies for maximizing your financial potential. By educating yourself on sound financial principles and strategies, you empower yourself to make informed decisions that align with your long-term financial goals.

Furthermore, embracing a mindset of abundance goes beyond just material wealth; it extends to encompassing a rich and fulfilling life in all areas. Cultivating meaningful relationships, prioritizing health and well-being, and contributing to causes greater than yourself are all essential components of holistic prosperity. True wealth is not just about the size of your bank account but the richness of your experiences, the depth of your connections, and the impact you have on the world around you.

In the pursuit of money mastery, it is important to remember that wealth is a tool to be wielded consciously and intentionally. By aligning your financial goals with your values and vision for a fulfilling life, you can create a harmonious relationship with money that serves both your personal growth and the greater good. As you continue on your journey towards mastering money, remember that true abundance is a state of being that emanates from within and radiates outwards, touching all aspects of your existence.

Being in service to others is the rent we pay for our room here on earth.
— Muhammad Ali

CHAPTER 10

Be Willing To Serve

Embracing Your Divine Purpose

As human beings, each of us is born with a unique purpose, a divine calling that guides us on our journey through life. Embracing your divine purpose means recognizing the special role you are meant to fulfill in this world and aligning your actions with that purpose.

To embrace your divine purpose, start by listening to the whispers of your soul. Quiet your mind and tune into the deepest desires of your heart. What makes you come alive? What brings you joy and fulfillment? Pay close attention to the things that stir your soul and ignite a sense of passion within you.

Next, reflect on your talents, skills, and strengths. These are the tools that will help you fulfill your purpose and make a positive impact on the world. Identify what you are naturally good at and how you can use these abilities to serve others. Your unique gifts are not random; they are the key to unlocking your higher calling.

Embracing your divine purpose also involves letting go of fear and doubt. Trust that you are worthy of fulfilling your purpose and that the universe supports you on your journey. Have faith in yourself and your abilities, and believe that you have been put on this earth for a reason.

When you align with your divine purpose, you are not only fulfilling your own potential but also contributing to the greater good of humanity. The ripple effect of living authentically and following your calling can inspire others to do the same, creating a positive impact that reverberates throughout the world.

Remember that embracing your divine purpose is an ongoing journey, one that requires self-reflection, dedication, and courage. Be open to growth and change, and trust that as you step into your purpose, the universe will conspire to support you every step of the way.

By living in alignment with your divine purpose, you become a beacon of light, radiating love, compassion, and positivity to all those around you. Embrace your uniqueness, trust in your journey, and know that you are here for a reason. Fulfill your divine purpose and watch as your life transforms in beautiful and meaningful ways.

Discovering and embracing your divine purpose is a spiritual journey that can bring profound meaning and fulfillment to your life. It is a journey of self-discovery, self-realization, and self-expression, where you uncover the essence of your true self and understand your unique place in the grand tapestry of existence.

Your divine purpose is not something that you can seek outside of yourself; it is a deep knowing that emerges from within, a calling that beckons you to step into your full potential and make a positive impact on the world. It is the intersection of your passions, talents, and values, aligning in perfect harmony to create a life that is rich in purpose and meaning.

As you delve deeper into your divine purpose, you may encounter challenges and obstacles along the way. These trials are not meant to deter you but to strengthen your resolve and deepen your connection to your true self. Embrace these challenges as opportunities for growth and transformation, knowing that they are guiding you toward a greater realization of your purpose.

At the core of embracing your divine purpose is a sense of interconnectedness with all beings and the universe at large. When you live authentically and in alignment with your purpose, you contribute to the collective evolution of consciousness, spreading love, light, and positivity to the world around you.

Your divine purpose is a beacon of light that shines brightly in the darkness, illuminating the path for others to follow. By living consciously and intentionally, you inspire those around you to do the same, creating a ripple effect of positive change and transformation that transcends individual lives and touches the collective soul of humanity.

Embrace your divine purpose with an open heart and a courageous spirit, knowing that you are part of something greater than yourself. Trust in the wisdom of the universe and the innate guidance of your soul as you journey toward a life filled with purpose, passion, and fulfillment.

Recognizing Your Unique Gifts and Talents

Every individual is born with a unique set of gifts and talents that set them apart from others. These inherent qualities represent the essence of who we are and can play a significant role in shaping our lives and our impact on the world. It is essential to delve deeper into understanding and cultivating these gifts to reach our full potential and contribute meaningfully to society.

Our gifts and talents can manifest in various forms – from creative abilities to analytical skills, from emotional intelligence to leadership qualities. They are like pieces of a puzzle that fit together to form a complete picture of our capabilities and potential. Recognizing and honing these gifts can not only bring us personal satisfaction but also enable us to make a positive difference in the lives of others.

To uncover your unique gifts and talents, introspection is key. Take the time to reflect on your experiences, interests, and innate inclinations. Notice what activities bring you a sense of joy, fulfillment, and effortless flow. Pay attention to the feedback and compliments you receive from those around you, as they often signify areas in which you excel.

Seeking the counsel of mentors, friends, or colleagues can also shed light on your unseen strengths and talents. They may offer valuable insights and perspectives that could reveal aspects of yourself that you may have overlooked or underestimated. Embrace this feedback with an open mind and a willingness to explore new possibilities.

Once you have identified your unique gifts and talents, it is crucial to nurture and develop them further. This can involve seeking opportunities for growth and learning, honing your skills through practice and dedication, and finding ways to apply your talents in meaningful ways. By leveraging your gifts to serve others and contribute positively to your community, you can create a sense of purpose and fulfillment that transcends personal achievements.

Remember, your gifts and talents are not merely for self-expression; they are meant to be shared with the world. Embracing and celebrating these unique qualities can lead to a more enriching and purposeful existence, enabling you to make a lasting impact on the world around you.

Furthermore, it's important to recognize that our gifts and talents may evolve over time. As we grow and learn, new aspects of ourselves may come to light, offering fresh opportunities for personal and professional development. By remaining open to change and adaptation, we can continue to explore and expand our potential, enriching our lives and the lives of those around us.

In essence, embracing and nurturing our unique gifts and talents is a lifelong journey of self-discovery and growth. By recognizing and celebrating the special qualities that make us who we are, we can create a meaningful and fulfilling life that resonates with authenticity and purpose. Let us continue to explore, cultivate, and share our gifts with the world, making a positive impact and leaving a lasting legacy that inspires others to do the same.

Cultivating a Spirit of Service

Cultivating a spirit of service goes beyond just acts of kindness or charity; it is a profound commitment to embodying values of empathy, compassion, and selflessness in all aspects of life. At its core, service is a recognition of our interconnectedness with all beings and a willingness to channel our energy and resources towards creating positive change in the world.

To truly cultivate a spirit of service, one must first develop a deep sense of empathy towards others. This involves actively listening to the experiences and perspectives of those around us, seeking to understand their joys, struggles, and needs with an open heart and a non-judgmental attitude. Empathy allows us to bridge the gaps between us and others, fostering genuine connections and a sense of shared humanity.

Compassion is another key component of service, as it moves us to take action in response to the suffering and injustice we witness in the world. It involves not only feeling for others but also feeling with them, allowing their pain to resonate within us and motivating us to alleviate their burdens in whatever ways we can. Compassion propels us to step outside of our comfort zones, confront privilege and power dynamics, and work towards creating a more equitable and compassionate society for all.

Selflessness is a foundational principle of service, encouraging us to transcend our own needs and desires in order to prioritize the well-being of others. It requires a willingness to put aside ego and personal gain, and instead, focus on how we can use our skills, resources, and influence to uplift those who are marginalized, oppressed, or in need. By shifting our orientation from self-centeredness to other-centeredness, we cultivate a sense of interconnectedness and unity with all beings, contributing to a more harmonious and loving world.

Furthermore, cultivating a spirit of service involves a commitment to social justice and advocacy. It requires us to be actively engaged in addressing systemic issues of inequality, discrimination, and oppression. This means speaking out against injustices, standing in solidarity with marginalized communities, and working towards creating a more just and inclusive society for all. Service is not just about addressing individual needs but also about challenging and transforming the structures and systems that perpetuate harm and inequality.

In essence, cultivating a spirit of service is a transformative journey that deepens our capacity for empathy, compassion, and selflessness. It calls us to embody these values in our thoughts, words, and actions, and to be a beacon of light and hope in a world that is often dark and chaotic. Through service, we not only uplift and empower those around us but also nurture our own souls and connect to a deeper sense of purpose and meaning in our lives.

The Impact of Service on Personal Growth

Service has a profound impact on personal growth in ways that are both transformative and fulfilling. When we extend ourselves in service to others, we not only contribute to the well-being of those in need but also experience significant personal growth along the way.

One of the key benefits of service is the development of empathy and compassion. As we immerse ourselves in the lives of those we serve, we are confronted with their struggles and challenges, allowing us to develop a deeper understanding of their experiences. This heightened empathy not only enriches our connections with others but also fosters a sense of solidarity and shared humanity. Through service, we come to realize the interconnectedness of all beings and the importance of supporting and uplifting one another in times of need.

Moreover, engaging in acts of service can help us cultivate a sense of humility and gratitude. When we witness the resilience and courage of individuals facing adversity, we are humbled by their strength and spirit. This humility encourages us to reflect on our own lives and the privileges we possess, leading to a greater appreciation for the blessings and opportunities we have been afforded. Through service, we learn to approach life with a sense of gratitude and to cherish the simple joys and moments of beauty that surround us each day.

In addition to fostering empathy and humility, service also provides us with valuable opportunities for personal growth and skill development. Whether we are volunteering at a local organization, participating in community projects, or engaging in advocacy work, we have the chance to expand our skill set and enhance our abilities. From honing our leadership and communication skills to cultivating our creativity and problem-solving capabilities, service offers a platform for growth and learning that extends beyond our immediate impact on others. These experiences not only empower us to make a difference in the world but also equip us with the tools and resources to navigate life's challenges and opportunities with confidence and resilience.

Furthermore, engaging in acts of service can serve as a catalyst for personal reflection and self-discovery. Through our interactions with others and our involvement in service projects, we are prompted to examine our own values, beliefs, and motivations. This process of self-exploration can lead to profound insights and transformative growth, enabling us to gain a deeper understanding of ourselves and our place in the world. Service encourages us to question and evolve our perspectives, opening up new possibilities for personal and spiritual development.

In essence, the impact of service on personal growth is far-reaching and multifaceted. Through our commitment to serving others, we not only contribute to the well-being of our communities but also embark on a journey of self-discovery, empathy, humility, and gratitude. Service has the power to transform us in profound ways, shaping our perspective on the world and enriching our lives with purpose and meaning. It is through acts of service that we can truly fulfill our potential and make a positive impact on the world around us.

Finding Balance in Giving and Receiving

As individuals dedicated to service, it is easy to become so focused on giving to others that we neglect our own needs. We may feel guilty taking time for ourselves or receiving help from others. However, finding balance in giving and receiving is essential for maintaining our well-being and effectiveness in serving others.

When we neglect our own needs, we risk burnout and decreased motivation to continue serving. It is important to recognize that self-care is not selfish but necessary for sustaining our ability to help others. Just as we recharge our phones to keep them functioning, we must also recharge ourselves to continue our service work effectively.

Self-care encompasses a wide range of practices, from physical activities like exercise and proper nutrition to emotional self-care such as setting boundaries and seeking support from loved ones. Taking time to rest, engage in activities that bring joy, and practice mindfulness are all ways to replenish our energy and maintain our overall well-being. By prioritizing our own self-care, we are better equipped to show up fully for others and make a positive impact in their lives.

In the same vein, being open to receiving help and support from others is a crucial aspect of finding balance in giving and receiving. While it may feel vulnerable to accept assistance, it is an essential part of building reciprocal relationships. Allowing others to support us fosters a sense of interconnectedness and strengthens our community bonds. It is through these connections that we can both give and receive with authenticity and humility, creating a synergy of mutual care and support.

Moreover, the practice of giving and receiving is deeply rooted in the interconnected nature of human relationships. Just as the ebb and flow of a river nourishes the land it passes through, the reciprocal exchange of giving and receiving sustains our emotional and spiritual well-being. By embracing both roles with grace and gratitude, we not only enrich our own lives but also contribute to a more compassionate and supportive society.

In conclusion, balancing giving and receiving is a dynamic process that requires self-awareness, self-compassion, and a willingness to both support others and seek support when needed. By honoring our own needs and accepting assistance from others, we not only enhance our ability to serve but also cultivate a sense of reciprocity and resilience that sustains us in our service work. Ultimately, finding this balance enriches our lives and deepens our connections, leading to a more meaningful and sustainable path of service.

Overcoming Resistance to Service

Facing resistance when it comes to serving others is a multifaceted and deeply ingrained experience that often stems from a complex interplay of psychological, emotional, and societal factors. These barriers to service can manifest in various forms, creating obstacles that hinder our ability to engage meaningfully with those in need.

One of the fundamental reasons for resistance to service is the fear of vulnerability and exposure. When we offer ourselves to help others, we open ourselves up to the possibility of rejection, criticism, and judgment, which can trigger feelings of inadequacy and self-doubt. This fear of being seen as insufficient or unworthy can be deeply rooted in our early experiences and the societal emphasis on perfection and achievement, making it challenging to step outside our comfort zones and engage in service work authentically.

Moreover, resistance to service can also arise from a sense of overwhelm and fatigue in the face of ever-increasing demands and expectations. In a fast-paced and competitive world, the pressure to excel and succeed can overshadow our desire to contribute to the well-being of others, leading to feelings of burnout and disillusionment. It is essential to cultivate self-awareness and reflect on our priorities to strike a balance between personal growth and communal service, recognizing that our well-being is intricately connected to the well-being of others.

Additionally, societal influences and cultural norms can exert a powerful influence on our attitudes towards service, shaping our beliefs about our role in society and our capacity to effect positive change. Messages of individualism and self-interest often dominate mainstream discourse, promoting self-centeredness and material success as markers of achievement. Challenging these dominant narratives and embracing a more compassionate and inclusive worldview is crucial to breaking down barriers to service and fostering a culture of empathy and solidarity.

Furthermore, resistance to service can also be rooted in feelings of unworthiness and imposter syndrome, where we doubt our abilities and feel like frauds when offering help to others. These feelings of self-doubt and insecurity can prevent us from stepping into our roles as compassionate and caring individuals, limiting our capacity to make a meaningful impact on the world around us. It is imperative to cultivate self-compassion and challenge the negative self-talk that undermines our confidence and sense of purpose in serving others.

In conclusion, navigating resistance to service requires a deep understanding of the underlying factors that shape our attitudes and behaviors towards helping others. By addressing our fears, insecurities, and societal conditioning with compassion and self-awareness, we can break free from self-imposed limitations and embrace a path of service that enriches not only the lives of those we serve but also our own sense of fulfillment and connection to the world.

Building Community Through Service

As a writer, my words have the power to transcend borders, cultures, and generations, leaving a lasting impact on those who have the privilege of reading my work. Through my books, stories, lectures, and podcasts I have the ability to shine a light on the complexities of the human experience, revealing truths and insights that might otherwise remain hidden.

When it comes to service work, building community takes on a profound significance that goes beyond mere collaboration or partnership. It is about nurturing connections and relationships that are rooted in empathy, compassion, and a shared commitment to making the world a better place for all.

In the realm of service, community-building is both an art and a science, requiring a delicate balance of strategy and heart. It involves not only bringing people together for a common cause but also creating a space where individuals feel seen, heard, and valued for who they are and what they bring to the table.

One key aspect of community-building through service is the cultivation of trust and mutual respect among all members. This requires a willingness to listen, learn, and grow together, even when differences of opinion or approach arise. By fostering a culture of open communication and inclusivity, you can create a community that is resilient, adaptable, and united in its pursuit of a shared vision.

Another important element of building community through service is the recognition of the interconnectedness of all living beings and the environment. When we acknowledge our interconnectedness, we start to see that the well-being of one is intimately linked to the well-being of all. This awareness can inspire us to work together, across boundaries and divisions, to address the root causes of inequality, injustice, and environmental degradation that impact us all.

Ultimately, building community through service is an ongoing journey of discovery, growth, and transformation. It is a process that requires patience, perseverance, and a deep commitment to building a world where everyone has the opportunity to thrive. By coming together with others who share your passion for service and social change, you can create a ripple effect of positivity and impact that extends far beyond what any individual could achieve alone.

Navigating Challenges in Service Work:

As a dedicated individual committed to serving others, you may encounter various challenges along the way. These challenges can test your resolve, push you out of your comfort zone, and demand a great deal of patience and perseverance. It is important to acknowledge that difficulties are a natural part of the service journey and can provide valuable lessons for personal growth.

One of the key challenges you may face in service work is burnout. Giving your time and energy to others can be emotionally and physically draining, especially if you neglect your own well-being in the process. Burnout is a serious issue that can impact not only your ability to effectively serve others but also your overall health and well-being. It is crucial to prioritize self-care and establish boundaries to prevent burnout. This may involve setting realistic expectations for yourself, learning to delegate tasks, and seeking support from others when needed. Engaging in activities that rejuvenate your mind, body, and spirit, such as exercise, hobbies, and spending time with loved ones, can help prevent burnout and sustain your passion for service work in the long run.

Another common challenge in service work is facing resistance or pushback from those you are trying to help. Not everyone may be open to receiving support or assistance, and it can be disheartening when your efforts are met with skepticism or rejection. In these situations, it is important to remain patient, empathetic, and understanding. By approaching interactions with humility and a willingness to listen, you can build trust and rapport with individuals who may initially be resistant to your assistance. It is also helpful to acknowledge and validate their perspectives and experiences, as this can foster a sense of empowerment and collaboration in finding solutions together.

Additionally, navigating the complexities of social issues and systems can be daunting. Addressing deep-rooted problems such as poverty, inequality, and discrimination requires a multifaceted approach and collaboration with various stakeholders. It is essential to stay informed, engage in continuous learning, and seek partnerships with like-minded individuals and organizations to maximize your impact. Building strong networks and alliances with community leaders, policymakers, and advocacy groups can amplify your efforts and create systemic change that addresses the root causes of social issues. By leveraging collective expertise and resources, you can work towards creating sustainable solutions that uplift and empower marginalized communities.

Despite these challenges, it is important to stay focused on the bigger picture and the positive impact you can make through your service work. Remember that every small act of kindness and compassion can create ripple effects that inspire others to do the same. By navigating challenges with resilience, determination, and a spirit of service, you can overcome obstacles and continue to make a meaningful difference in the lives of those you serve.

Navigating the complexities of service work also involves being mindful of the ethical considerations that come into play. As a service provider, it is essential to uphold the highest standards of integrity, respect, and confidentiality when interacting with individuals in need. Respecting the autonomy and dignity of those you serve is paramount, and it is important to prioritize their well-being and agency in all your actions. Additionally, being aware of power dynamics and privilege is crucial in ensuring that your service is equitable and inclusive. Acknowledging your own biases and striving to cultivate cultural humility can help you build authentic relationships with diverse individuals and communities, fostering trust and collaboration in your service work.

Furthermore, finding a balance between passion and boundaries is key to sustaining your commitment to service work in the long term. While your dedication to helping others may drive you to go above and beyond, it is essential to set boundaries to protect your own well-being and prevent burnout. Learning to say no when necessary, prioritizing self-care practices, and seeking support from peers and supervisors are important strategies for maintaining a healthy work-life balance. By recognizing your limitations and taking care of your own needs, you can continue to serve others effectively and authentically, making a lasting impact in the lives of those you touch.

In conclusion, navigating challenges in service work requires resilience, empathy, and a steadfast commitment to your values. By prioritizing self-care, building meaningful relationships, staying informed, and upholding ethical standards, you can overcome obstacles and create sustainable impact in your service journey. Embracing the complexities and uncertainties of service work with an open heart and a willingness to learn and grow can lead to transformative experiences for both yourself and those you serve. Your dedication to making a difference in the world is a powerful force for good, and through your actions, you have the potential to inspire others to join you in the noble pursuit of service and social change.

Creating Lasting Change Through Service

As we engage in acts of service, we have the potential to create lasting change in the world around us. Every small gesture, every kind action, every moment of giving has the power to ripple outward and make a difference in the lives of others. But how can we ensure that our efforts lead to sustainable, meaningful change?

One key aspect of creating lasting change through service is to approach our work with intention and a long-term perspective. It's important to look beyond the immediate impact of our actions and consider how they can contribute to broader, systemic change. This might involve advocating for policy shifts, challenging harmful societal norms, or addressing root causes of injustice and inequality.

Furthermore, embedding a sense of empathy and compassion in our service efforts is essential. By truly understanding the needs and experiences of those we seek to serve, we can develop solutions that are truly impactful and respectful of their dignity. Taking the time to listen, learn, and engage with individuals and communities can help us tailor our approaches to best meet their needs and aspirations.

Another crucial element in fostering lasting change is building trust and relationships with those we serve. Sustainable change cannot be imposed from the outside; it must be co-created in partnership with community members and stakeholders. By involving those most affected by the issues in the decision-making process, we can ensure that our interventions are relevant, culturally sensitive, and genuinely empowering.

In addition, recognizing the interconnectedness of social issues is key to driving systemic change. Many societal challenges are complex and interconnected, and addressing them requires a holistic approach that considers the intersections of issues such as poverty, inequality, discrimination, and environmental degradation. By working across sectors and disciplines, we can identify innovative solutions that address the root causes of these complex problems.

Lastly, promoting a culture of learning and reflection is essential for sustaining impactful service efforts. By regularly assessing our progress, learning from both successes and failures, and adapting our strategies based on feedback and evidence, we can continuously improve our work and maximize our impact over time.

Ultimately, creating lasting change through service is a multifaceted process that requires dedication, collaboration, humility, and a deep commitment to social justice. By staying true to our values, centering the voices and experiences of those we serve, and working collectively towards shared goals, we can contribute to building a more equitable, inclusive, and compassionate society for all.

Sustaining Your Commitment to Service

Sustaining your motivation and dedication is vital for the long-term impact of your work. In your journey, it is essential to cultivate a resilient mindset and nurture practices that keep your passion alive.

Reflecting on the impact of your service work is a powerful tool for maintaining motivation. Take the time to immerse yourself in the stories of those whose lives you have touched. Acknowledge the positive changes you have facilitated and the difference you have made in your community. This reflection not only reinforces your sense of purpose but also serves as a wellspring of inspiration to propel you forward, especially when faced with challenges.

Setting realistic goals plays a pivotal role in sustaining your commitment. Break down your overarching objectives into manageable steps, allowing you to track progress and celebrate achievements along the way. Adaptability is key in this process—remain flexible in adjusting your goals as circumstances evolve, ensuring that your ambitions remain aligned with your values and vision for impact.

Your community of like-minded individuals can serve as pillars of support on your service journey. Engage with fellow volunteers and advocates, share experiences, seek guidance, and offer encouragement. Building connections with those who share your passion for service creates a network of solidarity, empowerment, and understanding.

Prioritizing self-care is a non-negotiable aspect of maintaining your dedication to service. Nurture your physical, emotional, and mental well-being through practices that replenish your energy and foster resilience. Remember, taking care of yourself is not a luxury but a necessity to sustain your ability to give back to others.

Seeking inspiration from various sources can reignite your sense of purpose and reignite your flame for service. Delve into literature, attend workshops, participate in discussions, and explore new avenues of learning to expand your perspectives and cultivate fresh ideas. Drawing inspiration from diverse sources enriches your understanding of the issues you seek to address and fuels your creativity in finding innovative solutions.

Embrace the journey of service with an open heart and open mind, welcoming the opportunities for growth and learning that come your way. As you navigate the challenges and victories of service work, remember to celebrate your wins, no matter how small. Each milestone is a testament to your commitment and impact, deserving of recognition and appreciation.

In the depths of your dedication to service, may you find the sustenance and resilience needed to continue making a profound difference in the lives of others.

Bio

Coach Michael Taylor is an entrepreneur, author, (14 books) motivational speaker and radio show host who has dedicated his life to empowering men and women to reach their full potential. He knows first-hand how to overcome adversity and build a rewarding and fulfilling life and he is sharing his knowledge and wisdom with others to support them in creating the life of their dreams.

He is no stranger to adversity and challenges. He was born in the inner-city projects of Corpus Christi Texas to a single mother with six children. Although he dropped out of high school in the 11th grade, his *commitment to living an extraordinary life supported him in defying the odds.*

With persistence, patience and perseverance he was able to climb the corporate ladder of success and become a very successful mid-level manager of a multi-million dollar building supply center at the tender young age of 21. After approximately 6 years, he was then faced with another set of challenges as he experienced the pain and humiliation of divorce, bankruptcy and foreclosure, depression and homeless for two years living out of his car.

Bankrupt and alone, he committed to rebuilding his life which propelled him to begin a 25-year inner journey of personal transformation which resulted in him discovering his true self and his passions for living. As a result, he is now happily married (22 years) and living his version of an extraordinary life while being in service to others. Through his books, lectures and radio program he now coaches others on how to become genuinely happy with their lives and live the lives they were born to live.

www.coachmichaeltaylor.com
www.adversityisyourtally.com
www.creationpublishing.com
www.anewconversationwithmen.com
www.shatteringblackmalestereotypes.com
www.notokaywithgray.com
www.jesuswasacoach.com
www.joypassionprofit.com

Contact us:
Email: mtaylor@coachmichaeltaylor.com
Phone: 713-565-0083

www.ingramcontent.com/pod-product-compliance
Lightning Source LLC
Chambersburg PA
CBHW072156070526
44585CB00015B/1161